CHRISTMAS

ALSO BY JUDITH FLANDERS

A Circle of Sisters: Alice Kipling, Georgiana Burne-Jones,
Agnes Poynter, and Louisa Baldwin

The Victorian House: Domestic Life from Childbirth to Deathbed

Consuming Passions: Leisure and Pleasure in Victorian Britain

The Invention of Murder: How the Victorians Reveled in Death
and Detection and Created Modern Crime

The Victorian City: Everyday Life in Dickens' London

The Making of Home: The 500-Year Story of
How Our Houses Became Our Homes

FICTION

A Murder of Magpies

A Bed of Scorpions

A Cast of Vultures

A Howl of Wolves

Judith Flanders

CHRISTMAS

A BIOGRAPHY

THOMAS DUNNE
BOOKS

New York

Published in the United States by Thomas Dunne Books, an imprint of St. Martin's Publishing Group

CHRISTMAS. Copyright © 2017 by Judith Flanders. All rights reserved. Printed in the United States of America. For information, address St. Martin's Publishing Group, 120 Broadway, New York, NY 10271.

www.thomasdunnebooks.com

The Library of Congress has cataloged the hardcover edition as follows:

Names: Flanders, Judith, author.
Title: Christmas : a biography / Judith Flanders.
Description: First U.S. edition. | New York : Thomas Dunne Books/ St. Martin's Press, 2017.
Identifiers: LCCN 2017027330 | ISBN 9781250118349 (hardcover) | ISBN 9781250118356 (ebook)
Subjects: LCSH: Christmas.
Classification: LCC GT4985 .F58 2017 | DDC 394.2663—dc23
LC record available at https://lccn.loc.gov/2017027330

ISBN 978-1-250-19079-6 (trade paperback)

Our books may be purchased in bulk for promotional, educational, or business use. Please contact your local bookseller or the Macmillan Corporate and Premium Sales Department at 800-221-7945, extension 5442, or by email at MacmillanSpecialMarkets@macmillan.com.

Originally published in Great Britain by Picador, an imprint of Pan Macmillan

First Paperback Edition: October 2019

10 9 8 7 6 5 4 3 2 1

For Donna Leon

Legend

 Carnival and riot

 Drinking – and drunkenness

 Food and feasting

 Gifts and gift-giving

 The gift-bringers: Saints to Santa

 Greenery: The holly and the ivy

 Music and dancing

 Religion: Ritual and rite

A partial holiday calendar

January	1	Feast of the Circumcision, or Holy Name of Jesus
	5	Twelfth Night
	6	Epiphany
February	2	Candlemas
March	25	Lady Day
June	24	Midsummer
September	29	Michaelmas
November	1	All Saints' Day
	2	All Souls' Day
	11	St Martin
December	6	St Nicholas
	13	St Lucy of Syracuse
	21	St Thomas the Apostle
	25	Christmas Day
	26	St Stephen
	27	St John the Evangelist
	28	Feast of the Holy Innocents
	31	St Sylvester

When Mince Pies Reign

A history of Christmas might sound like a fairly simple undertaking. From nativity, to church, to family, to commerce – a story of high beginnings, a cosy, warm middle and the chill of cold cash at the end. That is how the story is often told. But is it the real story? For a start, every Christmas is different. The traditions of Catholic Spain are different from the traditions of Catholic Portugal and Catholic South America; Protestant Germany is different from Protestant Denmark, much less the differences between Protestant England and Protestant New England.

But religion, as we will see, is only one element – ultimately, and surprisingly, a small element – in Christmas as we know it. For there is Christmas the way it is celebrated in our own culture; Christmas the way it is celebrated in our own home; and Christmas the way it is celebrated in the mass media, in books and newspapers and magazines, on film and on television. All these Christmases are related to each other, but they are not identical. Because then, of course, there is that wondrous, nostalgically flawless day that is seared in our memories, the day that we can never quite recapture, the perfect Christmas. The poet C. Day Lewis got it right when he wrote, 'there are not Christmases, there is only Christmas – a composite day made up from the haunting impression of many Christmas Days, a work of art painted by memory'.[*] That is the key.

Each of us is a storehouse of Christmases, a repository of all the happiness – and sometimes sadness – of seasons past. Christmas is therefore magical: it enables us to be like Alice in Wonderland's White Queen, who could believe six impossible things before breakfast. We believe dozens of impossible things – often dozens of mutually contradictory things – about Christmas without even trying. Often without even realizing it.

For the holiday piles legend upon legend. Santa Claus was created in the Netherlands, or maybe his red suit was invented by the Coca-Cola Corporation; Prince Albert was the person to bring German Christmas trees to Britain; in the Middle Ages, the great feudal lords kept seasonal open house and fed anyone who appeared; the Roman Saturnalia was the origin of Christmas Day, or maybe it was the feast of Woden. Except – except, of course, that none of these things is true. At Christmas, and about Christmas, what is true, and what we think is true, is hard to separate from what we would simply like to believe is true.

The two most common assumptions about the holiday are, first, that it was religious in origin and second, that the traditions of each speaker's own country embody the real Christmas, the ones that others only palely imitate.

That Christmas was once religious, and only in our debased, commercial age has been reduced to its current shabby, market-driven modern form, is such a common

---

[*] Citations and notes for all sources can be found online at www. christmas-biography.com.

idea that it comes as a surprise when the actual make-up of the day is examined. First and foremost, of course, Christmas is the day established by the Christian church to mark the nativity of Christ. Today, therefore, we generally assume that the old Christmas – the real Christmas – was a deeply solemn religious event that our own secular, capitalist society has sullied.

The second assumption, that Christmas is native to 'our' culture, whichever culture that may be, is equally reflexive. To most people in Britain, in America, in Germany, Christmas is really a British, American, German holiday. Germans consider their Teutonic solstice myths, their trees, advent wreaths, seasonal markets, roast goose and red cabbage to be the authentic customs, the ones that produce a *Weihnachtsstimmung*, or Christmas feeling, that cannot properly be replicated anywhere else. The British and, in particular, the English, think their mince pies and plum puddings, their trees, their ghost stories and Dickens readings, their domesticity and child-centred festivities, to be the very essence of the holiday. In the USA, birthplace of Santa Claus and of Christmas stockings, of giant outdoor trees, turkeys and eggnog, Christmas is, just as obviously, American, and the rest of the world participates in their customs only by imitation.

And yet, even while we consider 'our' Christmas customs to be the true ones, we – most people in the West today who celebrate Christmas – in reality don't adhere to 'our' customs, but to an amalgam of traditions drawn primarily from the Anglo-American world and the German-speaking lands. These were then shaken up, mixed together with a couple of centuries of newspapers, magazines and books, not to mention a hundred years of radio, film and television, to end up not with one culture's Christmas, but with something entirely new, a holiday that is recognized across the globe, but comes from nowhere in particular.

And it is that Christmas, that strange hybrid growth that we all think we know so well, so well that we possessively refer to it as 'ours', that is the holiday, its history, myths, traditions, stories and symbols, that we will now explore.

Chapter One

The Bible is reticent on the birth of Christ. The nativity is mentioned only in the Gospels of Luke and Matthew. Luke was probably written around 80 CE, Matthew perhaps a decade later. Both may well have relied on a common source, for some details of their stories are identical. Luke describes how a census obliges Joseph to travel to Bethlehem, the city from which his family originates. There, Mary gives birth and her son lies in a manger, although there is no mention of a stable. An angel announces the birth to shepherds in the fields, who hurry to see the child. In Matthew, in the reign of Herod, Jesus was born in Bethlehem, as though this were his parents' permanent place of residence. Unnumbered, unnamed wise men from the east follow a star (no brighter, in this telling, than any other), bringing gifts of gold, frankincense and myrrh to the house where child lies. In the later, non-canonical protogospel of James, probably written towards the end of the second century CE, Mary gives birth in a cave, beneath a star that shines more brightly than the rest.

Historically, as is well known, much of the story as we have it is problematic. There was a census carried out in 6 CE, but that was ten years after the death of Herod, while there is no record of any census that obliged people to return to their place of ancestral origin to be counted. Further, these censuses enumerated property-owners. If Joseph owned property, why weren't he and his wife able to lodge there? And even if Joseph had to be counted, why did his pregnant wife go too, when women were not included in censuses? If Mary gave birth in December – and there is no mention in the Bible, nor in any early church writings, of the date of Christ's birth – why were the sheep still in the fields in the winter months, when they should have been taken in to the villages for warmth?

Moving from historical plausibility, it is likely that these writings made no reference to the nativity because birthdays carried little religious significance in the early church: the important day was the day of baptism, the day of religious rather than physical birth. From the second century, the Eastern churches marked 6 January as Epiphany, a Greek word meaning 'showing forth', indicating the day that Christ's divinity was revealed to man and, at least among some Egyptian Christians, the day was understood to mark Christ's baptism, although we have no knowledge of why that date was chosen.*

Constantine the Great extended tolerance to Christianity in the Roman Empire in 313; the establishment of Christmas as a church festival followed not long after. The earliest evidence we have for a celebration of Christ's birth is when Julius I, Bishop of Rome (337–352), decreed that Christ's nativity was to be observed on 25 December. Even so, from the start Christmas seemed determined to break away from religion: sometime before his death in 389, Gregory of Nazianzus, Archbishop of Constantinople,

---

* For a summary holiday calendar, see p. vii.

found it necessary to warn against the dancing and 'feasting to excess' that were occurring on the holy day. Nobody issues warnings about things that aren't happening, so we can therefore assume that, only thirty years after it was first mentioned, Christmas was already being spent as a day of secular pleasure. And so it continued. By the mid-seventh century, Theodore of Tarsus, Archbishop of Canterbury, was reminding his followers that while it was fine to eat well at Christmas, the church frowned on gluttony. It is difficult not to conclude that many were indulging on the day.

But why 25 December? According to biblical scholars' calculations, based on the Gospels and other church writings, 17 April, 29 May and 15 September are all more likely dates. The choice of 25 December seems instead to have been tied to the winter solstice, the shortest day of the year.[*]

No convincing evidence of winter solstice celebrations in pagan Europe has survived. Instead, the first instance of such celebrations that we know of was in Roman times, with three festivals clustered around this date. Saturnalia, when religious offerings were made to Saturn, the god of agriculture, began on 17 December and lasted for seven days. Work ceased, shops closed, gifts of candles were given and gambling, eating and drinking prevailed. This

---

[*]   25 December was the shortest day of the year when the Julian calendar was adopted in 45 BCE. Until the leap year was inserted in 8 CE, the reality of a solar year of 365.25 days meant that by 4 CE, Easter, calculated from the vernal equinox, had drifted away from its intended mooring. The vernal equinox was therefore moved from 25 to 21 March, and the autumn equinox and summer and winter solstices automatically moved too, thus unintentionally separating the winter solstice and Christmas Day.

holiday was followed by the Kalends, a secular, civic New Year festival, officially from 1 to 3 January, but often unofficially continuing to 5 January. Buildings were decorated with greenery and people ate, drank and watched races and processions, while small tokens, wreaths and garlands, or lamps inscribed 'Happiness in the New Year' were exchanged.

Libanius, a pagan Greek philosopher, described the Kalends celebrations of the fourth century, and they already sound familiar, featuring 'carousals and well-laden tables', 'abundance' for the rich, and for the poor 'better food than usual'. It was a time of spending: 'People are not only generous towards themselves, but also towards their fellow-men.' There was also a strong element of society turned upside-down, as masters waited on their slaves and senators dressed as plebeians. By the sixth century, wrote one Church father, these topsy-turvy traditions had prevailed, 'the heathen, reversing the order of all things', not just masters and servants trading places, but even men dressing as women. As with Gregory, two centuries before, he too worried that 'the majority of men on those days became slaves to gluttony and riotous living and raved in drunkenness and impious dancing'.

Between Saturnalia and the Kalends came the celebration of the solstice. By the first century, Mithraism had spread from the Middle East to become the most widely practised religion in the Roman Empire. Yet, despite its prevalence, we know little about it today. The central event is speculated to have been the slaying of a sacred bull by the god Mithras, probably a spring fertility ceremony. The *birth* of Mithras, however, was marked at the winter solstice, when, on the Dies Natalis Solis Invicti, the birth day of the unconquered sun, Mithras emerged from his birthplace in a cave, witnessed by two shepherds. By the third century, Sol Invictus was the main god of the Empire and Dies Natalis his primary festival, which now began to assimilate many of the Kalends traditions. This merging of holiday customs continued after Christianity became the established religion of Rome, in 380: 'when the doctors of the Church perceived that the Christians had a leaning to this festival [of Sol Invictus], they . . . resolved that the true Nativity should be solemnized on that day'. In other words, 25 December was chosen because it was already the commemoration of a sacred figure's birth. By the end of the fourth century, Eastern Christians in Constantinople were also celebrating Christmas on 25 December, rather than Epiphany on 6 January, as were Christians in Gaul. The holiday itself now expanded. In 567 the Council of Tours made the days between Christmas and Epiphany into a single holiday, which was confirmed by Alfred the Great in 877 in Wessex: his law code named the twelve days a general holiday, when even servants supposedly did no work.

In northern Europe, too, there were markers of the year-end. Most Germanic languages contain some form of the word 'yule', meaning midwinter. The Venerable Bede, in c.730, claimed that the ancient Britons called December and January Giuli, or 'Yule', but in the British Isles from the seventh century, Yule was used to mean Christmas.*

---

* Bede also wrote that there had been a pagan solstice festival called Modranicht, or Mother Night, but no other reference to it has ever been found. The word Christmas, or, rather, Cristesmæsse, Christ's mass, replaced Yule in the British Isles sometime after the ninth century, when referring to the liturgical date, not the celebrations around it. That word gradually became standard,

That Old English word, *Geol*, had derived from Old Norse *Jól*. Although today in Scandinavia *jul* means Christmas, originally it merely meant 'festivities', and we know little of these Norse ceremonies or beliefs. There may have been some form of ancestor worship, to mark the return of the dead, a not uncommon idea as the sun waned and the old year 'died'. Some said this was the day when in various northern European legends the 'wild hunt', that army of the dead, rode across the sky with their baying hellhounds led by Odin, or Wotan, on his eight-legged horse Sleipnir.*

Or it may have been a festival following the harvest and autumn slaughter, which was also the annual time for beer-brewing. The older oral tradition recorded in the thirteenth-century saga of the Icelandic bard Snorri Sturluson describes a midwinter festival of feasting and drinking, when the king *drikke jól*, or 'drank yule'. Bonfires and candles, or burning logs, as well as greenery, may have been part of the observances – we simply don't know. By 960 King Haakon of Norway had Christianized the day, decreeing that Jul was to be marked on 25 December, to coincide with the Christian festivities.

What can be said with certainty is that in the Christian tradition, from the early days through to the Middle Ages, many of the Christmas ecclesiastical developments were a matter less of religious liturgy than of entertainment. By the eleventh century in France, a star was hung over the

---

except in areas of Viking settlement, and Yule returned only in the nineteenth century, when the love of Olde England brought about a revival of what was then thought to be a relic of pagan days.

* In some places children left out straw, carrots and sugar for Sleipnir, but as carrots were not introduced into Europe until the eighth century, this is by necessity a much later contribution.

altar for an Epiphany play that was incorporated into the Mass, and the story of the Magi, of Herod, the Massacre of the Innocents and the Flight into Egypt, were acted out. In the twelfth century English churches also staged these plays, and as late as the sixteenth century church records show that painted and gilded stars continued to be made. Another form of theatre originated with Francis of Assisi, who in 1223 first produced a replica of a stable, with a manger, an ox and an ass. This became popular across much of western Europe, as did, in the Rhineland, *Kindelwiegen*, or cradle-rocking, services, where a life-sized cradle with a Christ child was rocked by the altar to the rhythm of *Wiegenlieder*, or cradle songs. In the Netherlands, two cradles, one on the altar, one near the congregation, were decorated with little bells that rang as they were rocked.

A distinctive seasonal feature in England was the miracle play. These plays were religious in content but, unlike Epiphany plays, they were in English, not Latin, and, unlike the *Kindelwiegen* or the nativity scenes, they were produced under the patronage of civic guilds, not the church. We know little about the early plays, but from at least 1392, guilds in Coventry staged *The Pageant of the Shearman and Tailors*, which recounted the events of the annunciation, the nativity, the adoration of the kings, the Flight into Egypt and the Massacre of the Innocents. A fragment of surviving stage direction indicates how the drama played out: 'Here Herod rages, in the pageant cart, and also in the street.'

One remnant of the topsy-turvy nature of the Kalends re-emerged in the European craze for the Feast of Fools, when minor clergy took over the roles of their seniors between Christmas and New Year. This was no gentle event:

> Priests and clerks . . . dance in the choir dressed as women, panders [pimps] or minstrels. They sing wanton songs . . . They play at dice [at the altar]. They cense with stinking smoke from the soles of old shoes. They run and leap through the church . . . with indecent gesture and verses scurrilous and unchaste.

Over time, these lewd games were replaced by a more innocent version of the servant-as-master inversion, this time controlled by the masters. 'Boy bishops', choristers who took on the bishops' role, were elected for the holiday cycle on 6 December, the name day of St Nicholas, patron saint of children, and they officiated especially on 28 December, the Feast of the Holy Innocents. The first boy bishop we know of was in St Gallen, in what is today Switzerland, in 911, and that this social upheaval was approved from above is clear: both King Conrad I of Germany and the Bishop of Constance attended services on the day the boy preached, the king attempting to distract him and his child attendants by rolling apples down the aisle. (The boys apparently turned a dignified blind eye to the misbehaviour of their rowdy adult congregants.)

Boy bishops were especially popular in England, many churches keeping miniature chasubles and staffs and albs for the use of their miniature clergy. Ultimately, Henry VIII took a dislike to the custom and it was banned in England in 1541. Queen Mary restored it, but it failed to outlast her, although schoolboys continued to enjoy St Nicholas's Day as a holiday. Elsewhere, it survived far longer. Many Swiss districts had a boy bishop as late as the mid-nineteenth century.

Churches saw more solemn pageantry on Christmas Day, but it was no less theatrical. Charlemagne was crowned the first Holy Roman Emperor on Christmas Day 800, and the holiday remained a favoured one for kingly entrances and exits: Edward the Confessor was buried in Westminster Abbey on Epiphany 1066, while the coronation of his successor, William I, took place the following Christmas Day. At Epiphany 1300, Edward I offered the church a gift of gold, frankincense and myrrh, a king marking the day of the three kings, a tradition that continued in England for another six centuries.*

The holiday impulse in courts across Europe, however, was primarily secular. Courtly feasting in Germany in the eleventh century saw guests singing secular songs (although at one of these feasts they were countered by liturgical chanting from the shocked clergy present). Welsh and Irish courts also held winter feasts from around the same date, and soon it was a time of feasting for all who could afford it. In Germany especially, year-end fairs became regular events, with one in Kempen being established from at least 1461 to supply these lavish entertainments. In England, rulers intermittently attempted to curb the excesses of the period, although with little success. Around 1100, Henry I

* By 1752, George II was merely going through the motions, and the ceremony was unimportant enough that a spectator felt able to mock the king's reputation for tightfistedness by noting that he offered only 'a small bit' of gold. By the 1850s Queen Victoria did not make the offering in person any longer, now dispatching the gifts via a servant, and a spectator dismissed the entire ceremony as 'a mere rag of Popery'.

issued a proclamation declaring the year-end a time of fasting, not feasting. Yet by the reign of King John, courtly Christmas feasts had become mind-bogglingly elaborate. On Christmas Day 1213 the king's household and guests consumed 27 hogsheads of wine, 400 head of pork, 3,000 fowl, 15,000 herring, 10,000 eels, 100 pounds of almonds, two pounds of spices and 66 pounds of pepper. Two hundred years later, Edward III tried again, passing laws restricting the meals on seven of the holiday's twelve days to two courses, with a limit of two kinds of meat per course.*

The recipes that have survived indicate that seasonal excess was not confined to the courts, but was also indulged in by the prosperous. One recipe for a Christmas pie from 1394 includes pheasant, hare, capon, partridge, pigeon and rabbit, livers, hearts and kidneys, and meatballs, all spiced and sauced and cooked with pickled mushrooms before being baked into a pastry case 'made craftily in the likeness of a bird's body', including a 'great tail' complete with feathers.†

---

* 'Course' is a modern word, and not quite equivalent to the structure of medieval meals, which were made up of 'messes', a series of dishes both sweet and savoury, all laid out at once. These were then replaced with a second messe, also of multiple sweet and savoury dishes.

† This was made for a feast at the Salters' Company in the City of London. By the seventeenth century the City's reputation for elaborate seasonal feasts had become a byword:

> The like was never seen . . .
> Men may talk of country Christmases, and court gluttony,
> Their thirty-pound butter'd eggs, their pies of carps' tongues,
> Their pheasants drench'd with ambergris, the carcasses
> Of three fat wethers [sheep] bruis'd for gravy to
> Make sauce for a single peacock, yet their feasts
> Were fasts compar'd with the city's.

This was the more remarkable, because from at least the fifth century, Advent had officially been a church-designated period of penitence and fasting, like Lent, with Christmas Eve a major fast day, on which meat, cheese and eggs were forbidden.* Yet the late fourteenth-century poem *Sir Gawain and the Green Knight* indicates that this was often honoured more in the breach. There, the castle guests are served

> a feast of fish,
> some baked in bread, some browned over flames,
> some boiled or steamed, some stewed in spices
> and subtle sauces to tantalize his tongue.
> Four or five times he called it a feast,
> and the courteous company happily cheered him along:

> > 'On penance plates you dine –
> > there's better board to come.'

That they are eating fish from 'penance plates' makes clear that this is a fast-day meal, but otherwise the notion of fasting is barely observed.

That feasting overcame all prohibitions is unsurprising. The European agricultural year almost dictated it. After the autumn harvest, grain was stored, fruit and vegetables preserved, followed by what the sixteenth-century poet-farmer Thomas Tusser called 'slaughter-time', when 'the husbandman's feasting begin[s]'. In the colder parts of

---

* The length of Advent was initially fluid, sometimes beginning as early as St Martin's Day, or Martinmas (sometimes Martlemas), 11 November. From the twentieth century, it began on the Sunday nearest to St Andrew's Day, or 30 November. For commercial, non-religious Advent calendars (see p. 169–170), it begins on 1 December.

Europe, St Martin's Day was the traditional time for slaughter, and feasting followed hard behind, with St Martin's geese or swine in Germany, geese in Denmark and Martlemas beef in England. In wine-growing regions, too, St Martin's Day was when the new wine was ready.

In England, seasonal drinking was given an archaic air, a sense of tradition to justify it. In the twelfth century, Geoffrey of Monmouth's *History of the Kings of Britain* told the tale of the fifth-century leader Vortigern, who was invited to drink with the toast, *Lauerd king wacht heil!* [more correctly, *wæs hæil*, or Lord king, your health], to which the response was *Drinc heil!* The story was almost entirely fabricated, and the parts that weren't were anachronistic by half a millennium. Nonetheless, this legendary *wæs hæil* was transformed into 'wassail' and became part of the holiday traditions.* In the fourteenth century the rich began to prize special wassail bowls of precious metals, using them for formal toasts; the poor carried humbler bowls from door to door, drinking to their superiors in exchange for food or drink.

As with the Kalends, by the Middle Ages the holiday period had become a time of gambling and gifts. In many places dicing and cards were limited to the Christmas season; in others gaming was legal year-round, but respectable people indulged only during the holiday. In one area in France, more than two-thirds of court cases concerning gambling occurred between October and February; in

---

* Although one folklorist has dryly referred to Geoffrey of Monmouth's book as 'one of our first historical novels', the word 'wassail' is used in *Beowulf*, in the eighth century, but simply as a toast, with no Christmas connection.

Castile, the royal monopoly on gambling was lifted on 25 and 26 December so all could indulge. In England, legislation permitted holiday gambling: by 1461, a law prohibited nobles from playing dice or cards in their own homes except during the twelve days; fifty years later, 'Artificer or Craftsman . . . Husbandman, Apprentice, Labourer, Servant at husbandry, Journeyman or Servant of Artificer . . . or any Serving-man' were all banned from playing 'at the Tables, Tennis, Dice, Cards, Bowls, Clash, Coyting, Logating, or any other unlawful Game', except at Christmas.*

With the twelve days considered a single holiday, the Kalends New Year's gifts became a Christmas custom. In *Gawain and the Green Knight*, the courtiers shout, 'Noel, Noel,' then

> 'New Year's Gifts!' the knights cried next
> as they pressed forward to offer their presents.†

These knights were offering gifts to their lord. Small gifts were sometimes given among friends, but more frequent were gifts designed to reinforce the social hierarchy, always given upwards, from knight to lord, from lord to ruler. In fifteenth- and sixteenth-century England, account books from the households of the great all indicate that

---

* Coyting was quoits, when a player tried to toss a ring over a stake set in the ground. In logating, or loggat, a spherical wooden shape was aimed at a peg. (It is from this that the idiom 'at loggerheads' originated.) I have been unable to discover what 'clash' might have been.

† In Norman French, 'noel' was originally an exclamation of seasonal happiness, as in *Gawain*. By the fifteenth century, the word had been transferred to the day itself as an alternative, if in English slightly affected, name.

gift-giving was routine, although we don't know how wide-spread the habit was lower down the social scale. In 1575 the soldier and poet George Gascoigne wrote that tenants traditionally gave their landlords capons at Christmas as part of a series of obligatory, year-round gifts:

> And when the tenants come to pay their
> quarter's rent,
> They bring some fowl at Midsummer, a dish of
> fish in Lent
> At Christmas a capon, at Michaelmas a goose,
> And somewhat else at New Year's tide, for fear
> their lease fly loose.*

In *Gawain*, after the gifts were given, the knights and their ladies 'danced and drank' for three days. Some great houses hired professional musicians, but more commonly, the entertainments were produced by and for the guests. In the fifteenth century a death in the family reduced one landowner's household to a most unseasonal quiet, with no 'disguising, nor harpings, nor luting, nor singing nor none loud disporting, but playing at the tables, and chess and cards'.

Thus by the close of the Middle Ages, for much of Europe, Christmas was certainly a religious festival, but while the church had included new traditions to mark

---

* In the British Isles, quarter days were the four days in the year when leases began and ended, rents fell due, servants were hired and school and university terms began. They were Lady Day (25 March, which was the start of the new year until 1752), Mid-summer (24 June), Michaelmas (29 September) and Christmas Day.

the day, it never succeeded in overwhelming the secular pastimes, and Christmas was primarily a time of 'feaste . . . where kynnesfolke do resorte together, bryngyng or sendynge presents mutually': food, family and giving.

Chapter Two

The focal point of medieval Christmas for the majority was not the birth of Christ, but eating and drinking and entertainment. For the rulers, however, the festivities offered opportunities beyond mere pleasure. By the sixteenth century James VI of Scotland, later James I of England, understood feast days to be tools of good governance, 'for delighting the people with publicke spectacles and for merriment' and, in so doing, displaying the might of rulers, entertaining their allies and impressing their foes with their wealth, all of which translated to power.

The music of earlier courts had rarely been seasonal. In the later fifteenth century, Edward IV's household included a 'wayte', a band of musicians who performed between Michaelmas and Lent. Several city corporations and guilds also employed waits to play at civic ceremonies, although it wasn't until the eighteenth century that their performances were confined to Christmas. But for the great courts' festive season, music alone was soon not enough, and to oversee the 'divers disguising and plays' that were coming to be expected at the holiday many of the courts of Europe appointed Lords of Misrule, courtiers, or men of social status, who planned the entertainments beginning in October and then acted as masters of ceremonies as they 'ruled' through the traditional twelve days and to Candlemas.

Twelfth Night, the eve of Epiphany, marked the end of the twelve days, and was equal to Christmas Day in importance. Imperceptibly in the British Isles, the title of the Lord of Misrule merged with the Twelfth Night's Bean King, who had originated in France. Bean cakes, cakes with a dried legume baked into them, had been sold in Paris markets from at least the thirteenth century. The recipient of the slice with the bean was crowned the *Rex Fabarum*, or King of the Bean, and was toasted by his fellow diners, 'The King drinks!' By the early fourteenth century the custom had travelled to England, and the courts of Edward II and Edward III both had crowned Bean Kings. Edward II's Bean King received a silver-gilt basin and ewer costing nearly £8 for his service. Edward III's Bean King was a Lord of Misrule too, organizing the king's entertainment and hiring his musicians '*in nomine Regis de Faba*', in the name of the Bean King.

The custom then briefly went out of fashion; pageantry did not. In 1377, more than a hundred wealthy citizens of London, accompanied by forty-eight men in livery, musicians, and men in costumes, 'with black visors, not amiable', rode out to salute the son of the Black Prince, presenting him with gifts of gold and jewellery, before being entertained to a banquet. In the fifteenth century, however, Bean Kings and Lords of Misrule reappeared: Henry VII had a Lord of Misrule and an Abbot of Unreason; James IV of Scotland had a musician King of the Bean in the 1490s. By 1509, the year of Henry VIII's marriage to Catherine of Aragon, the court allocated £450 on fabrics 'for the disguising' alone. The following year a portable stage built to resemble a hill surmounted by a gold tree was pushed down the hall towards the king as entertainers danced on it. In 1511 the king and a dozen courtiers performed a masque, combining dancing, music and dialogue, 'a thing not seen afore in England'.

Many of the greatest households had their own Lords of Misrule, as did civic corporations, colleges and other quasi-public bodies. Merton College, Oxford appointed a *Rex Fabarum* every November in the late fifteenth century, said to be 'according to ancient custom'. In 1545 the statutes of St John's College, Cambridge included a requirement that each of the Fellows was to take on the role in turn. The Inns of Court, great promoters of the holiday, spent heavily on year-end entertainment, and they regularly appointed a Lord of Misrule from among their benchers, or members.* One year, Gray's Inn's choice was commended as 'a very proper man of personage, and very active in dancing and revelling' – that is, he was suitable because he was both a gentleman and liked a good party.

Under Edward VI, the royal court's Lords of Misrule presided over extravaganzas on a scale rarely attempted before, not merely for the entertainment of aristocrats and courtiers, but also, as James VI and I was to later understand, to give people a sense they had a stake in the monarchy. Only seven month's before Edward's death in 1553, one Londoner described the Lord of Misrule and his retinue arriving by river at Tower Wharf, where they were received by the City of London's own Lord of Misrule

* Today the four surviving Inns of Court – Lincoln's Inn, Gray's Inn, and Inner and Middle Temple – are the professional trade bodies for barristers in England and Wales.

and his men. The King's Lord, 'gorgyusly a[rrayed in] purpelle welvet furyd with armyn, and ys robe braded with spangulls of selver', was accompanied by trumpeters and drummers, pipers, singers and morris dancers, and followed by mounted men in gold cloaks, with gold chains, each with their own retinues, fools, dancers, singers and pike-men. They marched through the City, 'trompet blohyng, makyng a proclamasyon', before the King's Lord gave the City's Lord a gold and silver gown, 'and a[non] after he knelyd downe and he toke a sword and . . . mad ym knyght, and after thay dran[k to each] hodur'. This was followed by a banquet, then a torchlight procession back to the river, where guns once more saluted the King's Lord as he took to the water.*

Christmas pageantry continued in London at the Inns of Court and among the City of London office-holders, who staged elaborate ceremonies. These, however, were not public, but events for members of the bar and their grand guests, or for the guilds and aldermen of the City of London. The Inner Temple held a breakfast on Christmas Day for their benchers, with 'Strangers of worth' invited to dinner; on St Stephen's Day the 'Constable Marshall' led a procession of trumpeters, fifers and drummers to kneel before their guest of honour, the Lord Chancellor. Other ceremonies were quasi-performances, as when a 'Master of the Game' and a 'Ranger of the Forest' hunted down costumed foxes, cats and hounds. These places also staged masques, which had arrived in the British Isles from, most

*   This type of extravagance could not survive the upheavals following the king's death. Edward's pageant overseer was the Duke of Northumberland, who unfortunately then backed the wrong heir, and his execution for treason put a damper on this festive role.

likely, France in the thirteenth century. (The first record was already one of suppression, when 'momment' – mummery – was banned in Troyes in 1263.) This courtly entertainment involved men dressed as angels, or devils, or gods and goddesses, or wearing headpieces of different animals, all supported by dazzlingly costumed squires and knights. The expenditure could be extraordinary: in 1633 the Inns of Court spent £20,000 on a masque entitled *The Triumph of Peace.**

For the majority of the population, however, mumming meant something far humbler, although for the earliest days we know little of what it comprised. Instead, much of our information comes from the ordinances that banned it: in the fifteenth century the City of London forbade anyone at Christmas to 'walk [the streets] by night in any manner mumming plays, interludes, or any other disguisings with any feigned beards, painted visors, deformed or coloured visages in any way'. In 1572 a banned St Thomas's Day parade in York was led by a personification of Yule and his 'wife' (the phrasing suggests that this was probably a man dressed as a woman), as their supporters threw nuts to the spectators. In Lincoln in 1637, a case was heard against a man who, dressed as a clergyman, had 'married' the daughter of the town's swineherd to a Lord of Misrule as his 'Christmas wife'. (It was impersonating a clergyman that seems to have tipped the scales against the offender.)

We know a little more about mumming traditions in

---

* Shakespeare's *Twelfth Night* was possibly also written to be performed on Twelfth Night, although the first performance we know of occurred on Candlemas 1602. The diarist Samuel Pepys attended a production of the play on Twelfth Night 1663, dismissing it as 'a silly play and not relating at all to the name or day'.

Scandinavia. In some districts people dressed up, mostly as animals, for a mischief night where pranks, or minor acts of destruction, were designed to incite fear or, at least, a pleasurable shiver of fear. These elements, together with some form of ancestor remembrance, make a strong link to our own Halloween, rooted as it is on All Souls' Eve, when the dead were thought to walk.

Another clue to early mumming forms may be found further afield, in Newfoundland, in Canada. In 1583 the adventurer Sir Humphrey Gilbert landed with five ships that had sailed from Plymouth, in the west of England, to claim part of the island for Elizabeth I. Four centuries later, customs that folklorists recognized from the West Country continued to be found there: morris dancing, hobby-horses and mumming. With no Puritan interregnum, as in Britain and New England, it may be that mumming in Newfoundland in 1962 was not too dissimilar to mumming in Bristol in 1487.

In some areas of Newfoundland, mumming was known as janneying, with big janneys (adults) and little janneys (children) disguising themselves in many layers of clothes or drapery; covering their faces with sacks, or fabric, or masks; and using assumed voices. Cross-dressing was routine, the women dressing as men and men as women, just as that horrified church father had reported in the sixth century. Sometimes hobby-horses, masks with snapping jaws, known locally as horsey-hops, accompanied the janneys.

The janneyers walked in a stylized 'jogging, half-dance, half-shake, that is the "mummer's walk"' as they went house-to-house, banging on pots or playing instruments. The householders then tried to guess their identities while the janneys attempted to foil recognition. This was followed by food and drink, music and dancing, before the janneyers moved on. Some roughhousing might take place: janneys carried sticks to keep those who would attempt to discover their identities at a distance, while householders might 'accidentally' trip the janneys to dislodge their masks.

Other rituals were recorded in the British Isles in the fifteenth and sixteenth centuries. Wassailing – carrying a wassail cup around a village or town to offer toasts in exchange for money or food and drink – occurred from at least 1461, when a church account in Hertfordshire recorded payments to wassailers. Soon it was traditional for young women to be cup-bearers over the twelve days, calling 'wassail, wassail', initially offering a drink in exchange for bread, cheese and mince pies, but from the seventeenth century mostly for cash.

These were asymmetrical payments, from greater to lesser. The practice of giving upwards, from lesser to greater, also continued. Monarchs, senior churchmen and others in power expected to receive costly items annually as thanks for their patronage, each gift calibrated according to rank and position: Elizabeth I's archbishops gave her gold worth £40, while lesser peers gave only £20. Lower down the scale, tenants continued to offer fowl or game to their landlords. In a morality play of 1578, a character thanks another 'heartily' for his help and promises to 'remember you every year with a Christmas capon'.

Hierarchical gifts were designed to emphasize status differences. While Elizabeth's courtiers never complained of their enforced gifts to her, complaints about the obligations of seasonal vails, or tips, to tradespeople and servants from their social superiors, were endless. The earliest reference is, as we now recognize as a pattern, a prohibition. In 1419, the City of London aldermen banned servants from soliciting Christmas 'offerings' from suppliers of food and drink to the Mayor and Sheriff's offices. Apprentices were said to have kept earthenware boxes, like modern piggy-banks, into which these tips were dropped; at Christmas they were broken open, and the term 'Christmas box' was transferred to the money. Soon the phrase had become proverbial: 'It is not for men to bee like swine, *good* for nothing till they be *dead*,' preached the President of Corpus Christi, Oxford; 'or like *Christmas-boxes*, that will afford nothing, till they be *broken*.'

Others asked for cash, but not for themselves. In the fifteenth and sixteenth centuries, in several rural regions of England, groups of hogglers, or hoggells, or hogners, or hogans, collected money at Christmas. We know almost nothing about them: we don't know what social group these men – probably men, although the sources are not explicit – came from, or what they did for the money, whether they performed a service, or provided entertainment. Church accounts indicate they made seasonal collections – from whom or how much from each we also don't know – which were then handed over for parish use.

Some of that money might have been spent on greenery: by the late Middle Ages in England, almost all surviving church records include entries for the purchase of holly and ivy in the winter. Private houses were also dressed with greenery, as were the streets themselves. In the early seventh century, Pope Gregory the Great had noted that decorating churches and holy places was a custom of the British Isles, although it was not yet seasonal: midsummer decorations were as common as mid-winter ones. One sixteenth-century historian claimed that in previous centuries every parish had a great pole serving as a maypole in the summer, decorated with holly and ivy in the winter, and that in 1444, a storm in London had blown down 'a standard of tree . . . nailed full of [holly] and ivy, for disport of Christmas to the people'.

This was not a Christmas tree as we know it, but it might be considered a precursor. For an association between trees and Christmas was emerging, especially in Germany. By the fifteenth century, the legend of the eighth-century St Boniface had become widespread. It told of an event one winter solstice, when the saint heard that a human sacrifice was planned under an oak tree, sacred to the god Thor. In a mighty rage, Boniface chopped down the tree, replacing it with a small fir, its evergreen branches representing Christ's eternal truth. (Awed locals were said to be so impressed by this analogy that they converted on the spot.) Another fifteenth-century legend told of a Bishop of Bamberg who witnessed apple trees miraculously blossoming on Christmas Eve. Soon sightings of miraculous Christmas flowerings were well-known.

Perhaps these stories were nourished by the popularity of the dramatic genre known in Germany as paradise plays. Christmas Eve was the feast day of Adam and Eve, and paradise plays opened with a scene set in the Garden of Eden, the tree of knowledge represented in midwinter by an evergreen fir with apples tied to its branches. After the plays went out of vogue, paradise trees continued to be erected in public places in German-speaking countries, initially on wooden pyramids, surrounded by ornaments and candles, and then without the pyramids, the ornaments and candles being tied onto the trees instead. As early as 1419, a Freiburg city guild erected a tree decorated with apples, wafers, tinsel and gingerbread.* In Reval (now Tallinn, Estonia), in 1441, what might have been a tree, or might have been a pole decorated with greenery, was erected outside the town hall, as in London three years later.

By the end of the century, trees or greenery were so common that Strasbourg passed an ordinance banning the seasonal cutting of pine branches; by the 1530s ordinances in Alsace limited each household to one small tree; two decades later Freiburg forbade chopping down trees at Christmas altogether. Even as these prohibitions were enacted to preserve forests, decorated trees were recorded with increasing regularity: in Riga in 1510, a tree was decked with 'woollen thread, straw and apples'; in 1570, a guild in Bremen erected a tree for their members' children to gather the apples, nuts and pretzels which adorned its branches.

These were public, outdoor trees, but by 1531 there was a new fashion, with Strasbourg markets selling trees for people to erect indoors, although these were apparently not yet decorated. The first decorated indoor tree we know of was in 1605, again in Strasbourg. Adorned with paper roses, apples, wafers, gilded sweets and sugar ornaments, it was what, a few years later, would be given a new name – a *Weihnachtsbaum*, or Christmas tree. These indoor trees were first recorded in the south-west of Germany, again around Strasbourg. It was later said that Martin Luther, inspired to thoughts of the goodness of God by the sight

* Wafers were small disks made of flour paste, generally used to seal letters or documents, but many of the early descriptions of trees included coloured decorative wafers.

of pine trees, had cut down a tree for his family so they could be similarly inspired. This is unlikely: Luther lived nearly 700 kilometres from Strasbourg, in Wittenberg, a town with no record of indoor Christmas trees until the eighteenth century.

Yet Christmas greenery was everywhere, and soon listeners were encouraged to 'Deck the Halls with Boughs of Holly', or at least they were in Wales, where the carol originated in the sixteenth century. The earliest Christmas music, dating from the fourth century, had been written by churchmen, for churchmen, and concerned the theological implications of the nativity. In the twelfth century, a carol was a secular French spring song accompanied by a dance.* In that same century, what might have been the first Christmas carol, 'Veni Emmanuel', was probably written. From the thirteenth to the fourteenth centuries, Christmas carols began to be written in Latin, followed by macaronic carols, with words in both Latin and the local language, and finally only in the local language. 'La Marche des rois', from Provence, may have been, in the thirteenth century, one of the very first carols to omit Latin entirely, along

---

* That carols were not restricted to Christmas can be seen in today's English usage, where we often say *Christmas* carol, despite it being vanishingly rare for a carol to be anything except a Christmas song. Defining a carol, however, ranges from the difficult to the impossible. The *Oxford English Dictionary* says a carol is 'A song or hymn of joy sung at Christmas in celebration of the Nativity', but this definition overlooks the hundreds of carols in praise of trees, holly, ivy, drinking and feasting, including 'O Tannenbaum', 'The Boar's Head Carol' and 'Deck the Halls with Boughs of Holly'. It also neglects the many carols that can more readily be classed as folksongs or ballads, such as 'The Cherry Tree Carol'. The simplest answer, perhaps, is that a carol is anything people decide is one.

with 'W żłobie leży' in Poland ('The March of the Kings' and 'In a Manger' respectively). In Italy, a Franciscan speciality was carols in which diminutives – *bambino, piccolino, Jesulino* – underscored the popular, childlike ingredients of the holiday and the song-form.

These carols all tell of the nativity. In contrast, the earliest English carol we know is contemporaneous with these but, unlike its continental counterparts, this Anglo-Norman contribution is a drinking song with only a token nod to seasonality:

> Lords, by Christmas and the host,
> Of this mansion hear my toast –
> Drink it well –
> Each must drain his cup of wine,
> And I the first will toss off mine:
> Thus I advise.
> Here then I bid you all Wassail,
> Cursed by he who will not say,
> Drinkhail!

Other carols involved holly, ivy or feasting. They were sung at court, in the streets and in private homes. In the sixteenth century, at the Inns of Court on the feast of St Thomas, the benchers processed and sang a carol as part of the entertainment.

In the middle of the fifteenth century Richard Smart, a Devonshire clergyman, may have written the first carol to greet Christmas not as a religious festival, nor as a season, but as a person:

> Nowell, Nowell, Nowell, Nowell,
> Who ys ther that syngeth so nowell, nowell, nowell?

I am here, syre Crystesmass,
Wellcome, my lord syre Christemasse

In the verses that followed, Sir Christmas oversaw eating and drinking and taught listeners the customs of the feast day, giving news of Christ's birth, but those lines were immediately followed with '*Buvez bien par toute la compagnie*. Make good cheer and be right merry.' Over time, the Lord of Misrule of the Tudor court came to be known as Captain or Prince or Sir Christmas.

Sir Christmas was a jolly innovation. Other personifications cast a darker hue. Winter was a time of superstition, of revenants, when the gods, or spirits of the dead, were more easily seen by the living. All Saints' Day and All Souls' Day may have evolved out of days when the dead were worshipped, or propitiated. With the dead came various intercessors, who rewarded or punished or blessed or banished their earthly followers. On St Martin's Eve, the saint handed out apples and nuts to good Flemish children, while in other places it was a wild man who did so, often the servant or travelling companion of a visiting saint, especially St Nicholas. These men might wear pelts, or animal skins, carry a whip or switch or crop, and be accompanied by some form of horse, or sometimes a goat, with a snapping jaw: Old Hob, Schimmel, Mari Lhoyd, the Klapperbock, Ziege, Habergaiss, Habbersack, hobby, hoden and the Julebukk, or Christmas goat, were a few of their incarnations.

There was a seemingly endless stream of these seasonal wild men, or elves, or ragged hermits, or devils, or some other form of outsider. Words associated with them were redolent of dirt (*schmutz*, *Aschen*) or class (*Ru* was rough,

Knecht a servant). *Pelz*, a common prefix, meant either fur, that is, animal skin, or came from *pelzen*, dialect for 'to beat'. There was Tomte [Elf] Gubbe in Sweden and Père Fouettard, Father Whip, in France; in Germany, Knecht Ruprecht, or Pelz Nichol, Ru Claus or Ru Paul, or Hans Muff or Hans Trapp, or Rumpanz, or Klaubauf (so called from his cry of *Klaus auk!*, 'Pick them up', as he scattered nuts and fruit in front of the household's children). There were more localized variants: Pelzmärtel or Schmutzbartel from around Lake Constance; Rüpelz or Butzmann in Swabia; in Alsace, Biggesel. There was also Aschenklas, Putenmandl, or Stämpes in the Rhineland and Semper in Bavaria. In Switzerland, there was Schmutzli and Samichlaus, a winter demon who carried switches to beat bad children and a sack to take babies away in. (More on the potently named Samichlaus on p. 105). In Austria, the Krampus was half-goat, half-demon, who ate bad children for his supper.* In the Netherlands, Zwarte Piet, black Peter, accompanied the saint.†

---

* There were a few women too, although not many. In the alpine intersection of what is now Germany, Italy and Austria, the Perchta, or sometimes Berchta, the wife of Odin, and occasionally the leader of the Wild Hunt, appeared on Twelfth Night. She was prone to slitting her victims' stomachs with a knife, replacing their organs with stones and straw. This fate could be avoided by eating Twelfth Night cakes or, in some regions, herring and dumplings, or pancakes. Other areas were visited by Frau Holle, or Frau Freen or Frick, which may be a link to the goddess Frigga. A few of these female apparitions cared for unbaptized babies, or rewarded diligent housewives, but usually they were women of fury, trailing havoc in their wake.

† Zwarte Piet is one of the few black helpers to have survived into the twenty-first century, regularly visiting Dutch towns and cities at

Whatever he was named, the wild man was ferocious. To draw attention away from these sidekicks to a Catholic saint, the Protestant reformer Martin Luther promoted a gentler idea, the Christkind, or Christ child, who gave fruit and nuts to good children. The treats were a constant in this season of food and drink. For like these legendary gift-bringers, legend – and rose-coloured spectacles – also tell us that Christmas was a time of extravagant hospitality, when the lords of the manor, and more minor gentry, opened up their great halls to strangers as well as friends, family and dependants, in an orgy of indiscriminate welcome and festivity. Writers of the period tell us this in all earnestness – or at least they explain that that was what used to happen, but no longer did. In their own day, they write, the great refused to spend time on their estates, instead frivolling away the holiday in towns and cities, leaving the peasantry without their lords for the holidays. In 'The Old Cap, or, Time's Alteration' a poet lamented the time when

> . . . Good hospitality
> > Was cherished then of many; . . .
> The holly tree was polled
> > At Christmas for each hall;
> There was fire to curb the cold,
> > And meat for great and small:
> The neighbours were friendly bidden,
> > And all had welcome true;
> The poor from the gates were not chidden
> > When this old cap was new . . .

Christmas. He is, therefore, the focus of modern discussions of racism, the many other black helpers having vanished into history.

The date of this verse is unknown, although it was in circulation by the 1620s. A cookery book of 1660 referred to this supposed golden age as one when the great fed the lesser, 'before good housekeeping had left England'. But did they? The evidence that survives, for the most part the account books of the very greatest households, indicates otherwise.

For example, in 1507 the Duke of Buckingham enter- tained 182 at dinner on Christmas Day, with another 176 at supper; at Epiphany, there were 319 at dinner, 279 at supper. But unlike later imaginings that suggest that at Christmas anyone could simply appear and sit down in any great dining hall, when Buckingham's guest list is exam- ined, his liberality is shown to be have a strong underlying political purpose. At Epiphany, most of his guests were local gentry or political supporters, together with their own followers and supporters; others were under his patronage, or they in some way owed fealty to him through political or familial affiliation. Of all those hundreds of people at his table that Christmas season, just three had no obvious obligation towards him.

Lower down the social scale, and absent the duke's political aims, comparable invitations of utility rather than of charitable hospitality can be found in gentry families. The majority of guests were the social equals of their hosts, whether friends or acquaintances, as well as those connected through ties of blood and marriage. When those of lower status were present, they were almost with- out exception tenants, or people who supplied goods and services over a long period. In this way, the gentry were systematically brought into contact with their dependants over the season, the meals building reciprocal bonds of loyalty. Even so, the lord and his immediate family usually ate apart, in a separate room, or at a different, higher table. Thus to interpret these large guest-lists as an indicator of a golden age of social levelling is to misunderstand what was a utilitarian review of those who would, in more recent days, be called employees. In modern terms, this was a CEO dancing with a warehouseman at an office party, not inviting him to her own family's Christmas dinner.

Senior clergy followed the same pattern, if on a smaller scale. In the early seventeenth century the Archbishop of York hosted a series of holiday dinners: for his tenants, then for gentry from the towns in his diocese, and after that for lesser ecclesiastical post-holders. Minor clergy followed suit, entertaining their parish clerks, the choir or bell-ringers, or other employees. Hungry strangers might, at most, hope for a loaf of bread at the kitchen door, as on any other day of the year.

The holiday menu was developing gradually. For the rich, there were already dishes that were considered spe-cifically Christmassy. In 1573, the poet-farmer Thomas

Tusser itemized:

> Good bread & good drinke . . .
> brawne pudding & souse & good mustarde withal.
> Biefe, mutton, & porke, shred pyes of the best,
> pig, veale, goose & capon, & Turkey wel drest:
> Chese, apples & nuttes . . .

As now, meat was the centrepiece of the holidays. Brawn had headed the list for centuries. Originally wild boar, later the term described a joint of pork, rolled, baked and soused either by being boiled in a vinegar broth or served with the animal's pickled feet or ears. Still later, a pig's head was boiled in a vinegar broth, the meat shredded and pressed into a mould, like pâté, and served with mustard. Possibly because it was no longer animal-shaped, there was some confusion in the Anglo-Norman period, and brawn was categorized as a fish dish, suitable for fast days, while still remaining a great celebratory dish – Henry V's coronation feast in 1413 featured brawn and mustard.

More flamboyantly ceremonial was a whole boar's head, which had been part of the Christmas feasts of the great from at least the thirteenth century. In the fourteenth century the Lord Mayor of London ordered the Butchers' Guild to supply a boar's head annually for the City Christmas feast. The famous Oxford 'Boar's Head Carol' was probably written in the fifteenth century, and by the sixteenth the boar's head and Christmas feasting were synonymous. Many later descriptions of it being served sound remarkably similar, as though one source were copying another: at some unstated but misty time in the past, a scholar of Queen's College, Oxford was attacked by a wild boar as he was walking in the woods, saving himself by thrusting his copy of Aristotle into its mouth, and remaining cool-headed enough to shout '*Græcum est!*'* He then retrieved his precious book by cutting off the animal's head, before having it served up to his fellow students. This implausible story was repeated routinely and regularly for centuries, with more or fewer embellishments as suited the teller.

The shred pies Tusser mentioned were, by the sixteenth

---

* This abbreviated form of *Græcum est; non legitur* – it's Greek to me – was presumably all the distressed student could manage while under swinish assault.

century, usually called mince pies. They were made of various types of minced, or shredded, meat, whether beef, mutton or veal, until the eighteenth century; then, as sugar became cheaper and more readily available, the pies became sweet rather than savoury. They always, however, contained dried fruit, including currants, raisins, dates and prunes, and possibly some fresh fruit such as apples and pears, and candied orange or lemon peel and spices.

Turkeys, when Tusser wrote of them, were a relative novelty, having first been brought to Europe from the New World by the Spanish in the 1520s.* Half a century after Tusser, however, they were commonplace: 'Capons and Hennes, beside Turkies, Geese and Duckes, beside Beefe and Mutton, must all die for the great feast.' The next sentence added that 'plummes and spice, Sugar and Honey, square it among pies and broth'. Tusser had made no mention of another Christmas dish, but even then, plum broth, or plum-pottage or porridge, was well known. Like the shred pies, it was savoury rather than sweet, a beef soup thickened with breadcrumbs and dried fruit. (An eighteenth-century Swiss traveller said very firmly that you had to be English to like it.)

In 1619 a masque at the Inner Temple featured a 'plump and lusty' Plumporridge, who fears that Master Kersmas (Christmas) is fading away. A doctor agrees: 'I

---

* Turkeys had an air of strangeness to them that became embedded in many European and Middle Eastern languages, where the word implies an origin in Turkey or India; in eastern countries, the point of origin is either thought to be somewhere in South America, usually Peru (as is the case too with Portuguese), or Europe, when turkeys became a French, Dutch or simply 'western' chicken.

saw him very lusty o' Twelfth Night', but while 'he may linger out till Candlemas . . . [he will] ne'er recover.'

No one could have foreseen how grievous the wounds Master Kersmas was to sustain in the coming decades would be, but somehow he would linger on long past Candlemas, biding his time.

Chapter Three

Sixteenth-century England had always had a few more religiously minded people, who forcibly expressed their concern about the drinking, gambling and what they saw as mindless pleasure of Christmas, instead of matters of life, death and afterlife. They were, however, a minority. Generally, those who wanted to reform the season were tolerated as eccentrics, their views nobody's business but their own, even as a number of Christmas practices were banned, or cherished, or banned once more as the throne passed from Protestant to Catholic and back to Protestant under Henry VIII and his successors. Under Mary, mystery plays were forbidden and boy bishops returned to favour; when Elizabeth sat on the throne, street plays gave way to mumming among the working people, while among the aristocracy, courtly masques gained new life.

Alongside these vacillations, a growing number of ardent Protestants began to condemn the secular holiday for a variety of reasons: that the holiday cycle commemorated saints, contrary to the Reformation's opposition to the role of saints as intercessors for mankind; that there was no biblical authentication for celebrating the nativity on 25 December; and, the familiar complaint, that the season was too much a period of licence:

> . . . The youth in every place doe flocke,
> and all appareld fine,
> With Pypars through the streetes they runne,
> and sing at every dore . . .

Edward VI addressed the problem of saints' days by sticking to the letter of the law: the Reformation had condemned the cult of saints, but omitted the apostles and evangelists from its wider ban. Thus the reformed church could still celebrate Christmas Day, St Stephen's Day, the Feast of the Holy Innocents, the Feast of the Circumcision and Epiphany, barely disturbing the traditional twelve days.

In Scotland, however, in 1561 the newly reformed Kirk declared all of Christmas a nasty popish invention and banned the holidays entirely. By the 1570s and 1580s, court records in the Lowlands (Highland practices were always looser, being further away from the centres of power) included a number of people condemned, or in some cases excommunicated, for marking 'superstitious days and specially . . . Yull-day'. Shopkeepers too were sanctioned for closing their shops, and guilds for marking the day. By the turn of the century, carol singing, playing football, 'guising' [mumming], making music and dancing were all banned as profane, although the quantity of ordinances against them is a strong indication that they persisted nonetheless.

In England, meanwhile, life was difficult for the nonconformists – those religious groups that did not adhere to the tenets of the Church of England and who did not acknowledge the holiday. One group travelled from East Anglia in 1607 to the Netherlands in search of freedom to practise their religion. Thirteen years later some set out again, this time on a ship named the *Mayflower*, heading across the Atlantic.

Earlier emigrants from the British Isles and France to the colonies in North America had taken the customs of their home countries with them. In the south, particularly in what was to become Virginia, the settlers were mostly adherents of the mainstream Church of England, and they observed Christmas as they had at home. Captain John Smith, of the Virginia Company that settled at Jamestown, spent December of 1608 among the Algonquian, 'where we were never more merry, nor fed on more plenty of good Oysters, Fish, Flesh, Wilde foule, and good bread, nor never had better fires in England'. Even in a wilderness setting, Christmas continued to be food, warmth and good company.

In the north-east, as the *Mayflower* travellers arrived in what would become Massachusetts, the holiday was to become contested ground. On the settlers' first Christmas in 1620, a mere six weeks after landing, work was obligatory, not for religious reasons but for survival. The emigrants were still living on board ship, and on the 25th 'we went on shore, some to fell tymber, some to saw . . . and some to carry; so no man rested all day'. On that day, they 'begane to erecte ye first house for commone use'.

Once shelter was no longer a pressing matter, however, fewer allowances were made. Yet the religious dissidents who had fled England and then the Netherlands in search of freedom of worship numbered just forty-one when they departed the Old World (seventeen men, ten women and fourteen children). They were heavily outnumbered by sixty-one other passengers, some servants of the Pilgrims, but many others simply hoping to find a new life in a new world. They had no interest in religious quarrels.

Thus, when some residents of the colony excused themselves from work on Christmas Day in that second year, professing 'it wente against their consciences to work on that day', it is likely that they were those 'strangers' who had also travelled on the *Mayflower*. Certainly the colony's governor, William Bradford, had no problem with permitting them to conform to their own practices – at least, until they were seen 'in the streete at play, openly; some pitching the barr and some at stoole-ball, and such-like sports. So he went to them, and tooke away their implements, and tould them that it was against his conscience that they should play and others worke. If they made the keeping of [Christmas] a mater of devotion, let them kepe their houses, but ther should be no gameing or revelling in the streets.'

A unified population, all sharing identical beliefs, was never a reality in the colonies. New France covered not only much of what later became Canada, but also a great swathe of territory down to the Gulf of Mexico, and the French settlers maintained their own holiday traditions: on the religious side, midnight Mass; on the secular, good food and drink. In the 1620s and 1630s Samuel de Champlain, Governor of New France, presided over feasts of venison, squirrel and wildfowl, both stewed and in pies, eel and salmon, and sweet dishes baked with maple-sugar, that new-world culinary innovation.

In the 1630s, a further 20,000 immigrants settled in New England, bringing their own customs. Possibly it was this numerical imbalance that caused the Puritans to tighten their grip: they may have felt that they had not travelled all that way, in such peril, to be surrounded by those whose practices were so at odds with their own. Or it may have been that events in England and Scotland had given them hope that their own views could be made to prevail.

James VI of Scotland's love of holiday celebrations had been a problem for the Kirk, ensuring Christmas bans were impossible during his reign. When he gained the throne of England too, in 1603, with its populace more tolerant of the secular holiday, it must have seemed to the Puritans that the battle was lost. In 1617 the king attempted to enforce legally the celebration of the twelve days. Yet this was only ever partially successful; after his death in 1625 the monarchy lost even the appearance of control in Scotland, and in 1638 the General Assembly banned Christmas outright. Gradually, even gestures towards the holiday were liable to punishment.

Initially, this was in marked contrast to England. Half a decade after the ill-suited Charles I succeeded James, Christmas continued to be a time of festivity and enjoyment. One 'lesson' instructed young men to 'Be holy in Lent. Be [painstaking] in Harvest. Be merry at Christmas.' Even churchmen agreed: Christmas was, said the Bishop of Winchester, a 'season of gathering together, of neighbourly meetings and invitations . . . of good housekeeping and hospitality'. But once the Civil War began, there was no longer any space for neighbourly gatherings. Now what mattered were the views of reformers, who saw Christmas, unmentioned in the Bible, as a mark of the antichrist. At first their attacks on the day concentrated on its secular elements, and in 1642 Parliament banned seasonal plays. But in 1643, when the Long Parliament joined forces with the Scottish government, all holiday observances, secular and religious, were forbidden. Parliament sat on 25 December, to make sure the people understood that this was a working day like any other, and by 1645 'Festival days, vulgarly called Holy days, having no Warrant in the Word of God, are not to be continued.'

Not everyone agreed. While the regime demanded that shops stay open, some apprentices forced their masters to close: in 1646 in Bury St Edmunds, they took to the streets, and further scuffles and fights broke out the next year too, with a 'great mutiny' in Norwich, while in Canterbury a mob demanding holiday church services attacked the mayor's house. Christmas traditions became symbols of the royalist cause. 'Christmas was kil'd at *Nasbie* fight', claimed one broadside: 'Charity was slain . . . Likewise then did die, / Rost beef and shred pie.'* In London in 1647, there was a tense stand-off when now-illicit greenery was defiantly hung on City walls. The Lord Mayor and City Marshal rode out to supervise its removal, but their calls for ladders went unheeded by an angry crowd, who spooked the mayor's horse, making it bolt – or, as a royalist pamphlet gleefully interpreted the episode, 'The pulling down of holly and ivy was an act his very horse was ashamed of.'

Royalists, and the more conservative Church of England worshippers, tried to mark the day, either in secular or religious form, but it was difficult, and sometimes dangerous. In 1652, with churches forced to close, the diarist John Evelyn found, 'no Sermon anywhere, so observ'd [Christmas Day] at home'. The following year was the same: 'No churches[, nor] publique Assembly, I was faine

---

* Charles I lost the Battle of Naseby decisively to Cromwell, leading to the Parliamentarians' ultimate victory in the Civil War.

to passe the devotions of that blessed day with my family at home.' 1654 was worse, with penalties levied on anyone who attempted to worship in church. In 1655 all Church of England ministers were barred from both teaching and preaching, and after that, wrote Evelyn, 'There was no more notice taken of Christmas Day in Churches.' The following year saw Evelyn attend a service at the Earl of Rutland's private chapel, held in defiance of parliamentary orders, but as the clergyman 'was giving us the holy Sacrament, The Chapell was surrounded with Souldiers: all the Communicants and Assembly surpriz'd and kept Prisoner'. Evelyn was held and questioned as to

> why contrarie to an Ordinance made that none should any longer observe the superstitious time of the Nativity (so esteem'd by them), I durst offend and particularly be at Common prayers, which they told me was but the Masse in English [that is, was Catholic in all but name], and particularly pray for Charles stuard, for which we had no Scripture: I told them we did not pray for Ch: Steward, but for all Christian Kings, Princes and Governors: The[y] replied, in so doing we praied for the K[ing] of Spaine too, who was their Enemie, and a Papist, with other frivolous and insnaring questions, with much threatning . . .

While Evelyn was attempting to worship, many more were battling governmental regulations over secular customs. Shops now closed on 25 December because the day routinely provoked street disorder. But this had consequences unforeseen by either reformers or royalists as, with shops and churches closed, and private celebrations under a cloud, people went to inns and taverns and drank. The banning of Christmas by religious reformers had ensured that the day became ever more secular.

Banning Christmas celebrations, however, is not the same as Christmas celebrations being banned. In 1659 the Massachusetts Bay court instituted 5s. fines for anyone caught 'forbearing of labour, feasting', or celebrating the day 'in any other way', yet court records show that in the twenty-two years the law was in force, not a single person was brought up on charges of enjoying Christmas. Given the region's many non-Puritans, it is impossible that no one marked the day. Perhaps, instead, celebrating Christmas in Puritan New England should be understood to be like speeding in the twenty-first century. When drivers stick to 23 or 24 mph in a 20 mph zone, a blind eye is turned; if they drive at 40 mph, it is more likely they will be arrested. As long as holiday celebrations were private, participants could expect no repercussions.

Whatever the case, the ban could not long survive the political revolution that was the death of Cromwell and the end of parliamentary rule back in England. There, following the Restoration of the monarchy in 1660, all parliamentary legislation passed after 1637 was formally revoked. North of the border, however, the Scottish Kirk continued to frown on the holiday that was being relegitimated in the south, and in 1690 it reinstated its ban.*

In the Massachusetts Bay colony, the ruling caste was no more open to the holiday. It took a foot-dragging two decades for it to comply with London's order to lift the

---

* This ban survived until 1958, when Christmas became an official holiday in Scotland for the first time in a quarter of a millennium.

ban, only doing so finally in 1681. In England, even many who had professed Puritan ideals from conviction, rather than expediency, now simply took pleasure in the season. One nonconformist vicar, who had been an ardent Commonwealthman, could stand in for many on Christmas Day 1667 as he 'feasted. [his] Tenants and all [his] children with joy'.

Most of his countrymen felt the same, returning to the old ways, eating, dancing, drinking, playing cards and games, singing and telling stories. Some, however, especially those who had supported the monarchy, began to develop an interest in what they identified as special Christmas observances, things that people did at that time of year and no other, the power of ritual making a political as well as religious point.

The poet Robert Herrick was a vicar in Devonshire for just over fifteen years, and many of his poems referred to the customs of the people. Historians and folklorists have since mined them for information on the holiday, for his are often the first surviving references we have to a number of traditions. It is important therefore to look not merely at what Herrick wrote, but why he wrote it.

Herrick's childhood home was Calvinist, but moderate, and his London merchant family celebrated Christmas in 'good will in feasting', enjoying 'musike', eating Christmas 'porredge and pyes'. By the 1640s Herrick had become an outspoken monarchist, publishing poems in praise of the doomed Charles I. His major collection of poetry, *Hesperides*, begins with a verse setting out his aim to hymn the customs of the rural people, and also of 'The Court of

Mab, and of the Fairie-King' – that is of both the real and the imaginary worlds. In extolling the country-people's wakes, morris dancing, Whitsun ale, harvest and shearing feasts, wassailing, mumming and Twelfth Night kings and queens, he was also making a political point: his list of subjects was virtually identical to those praised by James I, emphasizing what would vanish if the royalists were to lose the Civil War.

Sometimes separating fact from imagination in Herrick's work is relatively straightforward. In 'The Wassaile', Herrick's wassailers ask for beer in exchange for blessings. The estate they call at is not a wealthy, thriving manor house, but a ghost of itself, a vision of disrepair brought about by newfangled ideas. Yet the practice of wassailing was recorded enough elsewhere that we can compare and contrast his poems with other sources.

There were two types of wassailing. In one, working people went house to house, toasting the residents in exchange for money, or beer, or food. In the second, agricultural workers toasted their orchards, to promote good harvests in the following year:

> Wassaile the Trees, that they may beare
> You many a Plum, and many a Peare:
> For more or lesse fruits they will bring,
> As you doe give them Wassailing.

Herrick's account of wassailing of trees corresponds with another, from Sussex in the 1660s or 1670s, in which boys 'howl' (possibly a corruption of Yule) the orchards. The antiquary John Aubrey, in a near-contemporaneous study, recorded the same practice in Yorkshire.

Herrick also described the lighting the 'Christmas Log'

from a saved piece of the previous year's log, for luck. This is the first surviving mention, although burning a large log at Christmas had been customary in parts of Germany for some centuries, and may have been the origin of the English tradition. Again, other sources vouch for the practice elsewhere in the country: in 1648, John Taylor, the 'Water Poet' (he was a waterman on the Thames), lamented the custom's decline in the capital; twenty years later, Aubrey found it flourishing in Yorkshire.

Herrick is also the first source to associate mistletoe with the holiday, in his 'Ceremonie upon Candlemas Eve', the day Christmas greenery was removed: 'Down with the Rosemary, and so / Down with the Baies, & mistletoe'. Once more Taylor echoed Herrick's account, and the herbalist William Coles mentioned it soon afterwards. What we don't know was whether Christmas mistletoe was a seventeenth-century novelty, or if earlier references to it just failed to survive, or had never been written down. Nor can we say where it was in use. Taylor wrote almost entirely about London, where Herrick had also spent much of his life. Herrick was in Devonshire when he wrote of the custom, but that does not mean that that was where he saw it.

When Herrick becomes our sole, or most detailed, source, matters become even less certain. In 'Christmasse-Eve, another Ceremonie' Herrick describes what sounds like a long-established practice:

> Come guard this night the Christmas-Pie,
> That the Thiefe, though ne'r so slie,
> With his Flesh-hooks, don't come nie
> To catch it.

Yet no one else records anything remotely like this. Perhaps the poem is a political allegory; Herrick would not be alone in writing about politics in holiday disguise. Ben Jonson's 1616 *Christmas, His Masque* also comments on the current political turmoil: a character named variously Old Christmas, Christmas of London and Captain Christmas affirms that, although he was born in Pope's Head Alley (a real London street as well as a nod to the Puritan belief that Christmas was a 'popish' day), he is 'as good a Protestant as any'. His ten children, Misrule, Carol, Mince Pie, Gambol, Post-and-Pair (a card game), New Year's Gift, Mumming, Wassail, Offering (charitable giving) and Baby Cake (another name for a Twelfth Night, or bean cake), were personifications of Christmas practices 'of old', looking back to an ideal Christmas that was no more.

Personifying the holiday became a favoured tool of promoters of the season, be it using him as a 'King of good cheer and feasting' or turning him into an old man behind bars under the Commonwealth.

The first personification had appeared at least a century earlier. It was, however, in Alsace, not in England, that the Weihnachtsmann, the Christmas Man, first emerged in the early sixteenth century. He was followed by the Christkind, introduced in Protestant regions by Martin Luther. Initially a devout holy child, by the nineteenth century the Christkind had softened, becoming an angelic blond, girlish figure in a white dress, wearing a gold crown surmounted by a candle. Sometimes he was smaller, more childlike, and called the Christpuppe, or Christ-doll. But neither could compete in ubiquity with St Nicholas and his accompanying helper.

The St Nicholas legend had developed in the Netherlands when it was under Spanish occupation between 1581 and 1714. There, by the seventeenth century, St Nicholas was accompanied by his Moorish helper, Zwarte Piet, as he deposited small presents in the shoes of good children, leaving it to Zwarte Piet to mete out punishment to the bad. Elsewhere on the continent, St Nicholas had earlier handed out apples and nuts, symbols of harvest and plenty; it is possible that oranges were now added in this country ruled by the princes of the House of Orange-Nassau.* So were baked goods: honey cake and a spice cake called parliament bread were sold seasonally across the Netherlands, while in Dordrecht, a *claescoeck*, or Nicholas cake, was a regional speciality.

Such gifts of food were becoming common, whether given by St Nicholas, the Christkind or the Weihnachtsmann, even as the custom of presenting gifts to show loyalty to a feudal lord were dying away as feudalism itself was dying. In England, Old Christmas had not been a gift-bringer, but there gifts of obligation continued for a time. The diarist Samuel Pepys recorded that his patron, the Earl of Sandwich, commander of the fleet that brought Charles II back to England, had as 'an Earle [given] 20 pieces in gold in a purse to the King', 'as is usuall at this time of the year'. Soon, however, the destabilized monarchy finished the custom off: it was rumoured, and may have been true, that Charles II had turned all of his gifts over to one of his

* However, by the eighteenth century, oranges were also being given as year-end gifts by people in England and in the colonies, so it may have been a happy coincidence, later worked into something more significant.

mistresses, making an already unpopular requirement less popular still.

By contrast, gift-giving between equals increased. In the Netherlands there were *sanctjes*, little cards bearing an image of St Nicholas. In France and in England, for the increasing numbers of the literate, books were becoming the standard gift, and would remain so, while in England small items of jewellery, wine and luxury foods also came into vogue. Food and drink dominated: in 1660 Pepys recorded receiving a turkey from an old friend, a bird from the country remaining a frequent year-end gift throughout the nineteenth century and into the twentieth. He also received a dozen bottles of sack (white wine) from his patron.

This latter was not, of course, a gift between equals. Lord Sandwich was a member of the Council of State and a peer; Pepys was a naval administrator – a civil servant. And this quasi-gift – a tip, or top-up to payments made throughout the year, was, and was to remain, a seasonal staple. It also remained, for the giver, a source of seasonal grumbling. When Christmas was forbidden, wrote John Taylor, apprentices and servants, deliverymen and boys were all out of luck: 'their Christmas Boxes were banished' too. With the return of the monarchy came the return of Christmas boxes. When Pepys paid his shoemaker, he automatically 'gave something to the boy's box against Christmas'; another year, he 'dropped money at five or six places, which I was the willinger to do, it being Christmas Day'.

It was literally Christmas Day, 25 December, when Pepys made these payments: the shops were all open. For half a century closed shops had indicated Christmas observance; now open shops meant the same, because Christmas was the time of eating and drinking, and some foods had to be purchased on the day of consumption.

Pepys's Christmas dinner in 1662 had included a mince pie, a 'brave plum-porridge and a roasted Pullet', the sort of winter meal that a family of middle income would expect. By contrast, great houses still served up great feasts. The first major cookbook in English giving household recipes set out in 1660 'A Bill of Fare for Christmas Day':

Oysters.

1. A collar of brawn.

2. Stewed Broth of Mutton marrow bones.

3. A grand Sallet.

4. A pottage of caponets.

5. A breast of veal in stofado.

6. A boil'd partridge.

7. A chine of beef, or surloin roast.

8. Minced pies.

9. A Jegote [gigot] of mutton with anchove sauce.

10. A made dish of sweetbread.

11. A swan roast.

12. A pasty of venison.

13. A kid with a pudding in his belly.

14. A steak pie.

15. A haunch of venison roasted.

16. A turkey roast and stuck with cloves.

17. A made dish of chickens in puff paste.

18. Two bran geese roasted, one larded.

19. Two large capons, one larded.

20. A custard.

The second course for the same Mess.

Oranges and Lemonds.

21. A young lamb or kid.

22. Two couple of rabbits, two larded.

23. A pig souc't with tongues.

24. Three ducks, one larded.

25. Three pheasants, 1 larded.

26. A Swan Pye.

27. Three brace of partridge, three larded.

28. Made dish in puff paste.

29. Bolonia sausages, and anchovies, mushrooms, and Cavieate, and pickled oysters in a dish.

30. Six teels, three larded.

31. A Gammon of Westphalia Bacon.

32. Ten plovers, five larded.

33. A quince pye, or warden pie.

34. Six woodcocks, 3 larded.

35. A standing Tart in puff paste, preserved fruits, Pippins, &c.

36. A dish of Larks.

37. Six dried neats [ox] tongues.

38. Sturgeon.

39. Powdered Geese. Jellies.

With this went music, for 'the Holidayes and Musicke . . . must bee in tune', 'and not a Cup of drinke must passe without a Caroll'. In carols, food and drink were linked, with many lyrics giving at most a nod to religion before turning to more important things:

> Now that the time is come wherein
> Our Saviour Christ was born,
> The larders full of beef and pork,
> And garners filled with corn . . .

These carols were now everywhere. The very first collection had been English, in 1521, but after that, carol publishing moved to continental Europe. One of the most influential collections was compiled by the head of the cathedral school in Turku, in what is now Finland, in 1582. Entitled *Piae Cantiones Ecclesiasticae et Scholasticae Veterum Episcoporum* (Pious Church and School Songs of the Ancient Churchmen), it was a collection of seventy-three Latin hymns and carols sung in Germany, England, France, Sweden, Finland and Italy, together with their tunes.* More carols were written in the languages of each country. By the end of the seventeenth century, the following were all known: 'Deck the Halls with Boughs of Holly', 'The First Nowell', 'God Rest You Merry, Gentlemen', 'We Wish You a Merry Christmas', 'The Cherry Tree Carol', 'The Coventry Carol' and 'The Somerset Carol' in the British Isles; in Poland 'Lulajże Jezuniu' (the melody of which was adapted by Chopin in his first Scherzo, in 1830); in Germany, 'Vom Himmel hoch, da komm' ich her', written by Luther himself, and parts of 'O Tannenbaum'

---

* One of these tunes was repurposed, with new lyrics, in Britain in 1853, and became 'Good King Wenceslas'. As with early carols more generally, a number of songs included here were not for Christmas at all.

(the first verse and musical setting are probably sixteenth or seventeenth century, the later verses and musical adaptation are nineteenth century); and in Sweden, 'Nu är det Jul igen', to name but a few. New France had 'Jesous Ahatonhia', its first indigenous-language carol, written by the missionary Father Jean de Brébeuf in Huron (Wyandot), in which Jesus lies in a birchbark lodge as great chiefs from afar come bearing beaver pelts.

The lyrics of carols could encompass the nativity, Christmas greenery, or love, or they could be comic verses, or political satire. One 1675 carol booklet, 'Make Room for Christmas All you that do love Him', outlined a tradesman's Christmas: visiting neighbours, roasting apples by the fire, listening to a merry tale, singing 'melodious Carrols', and 'so we'l be higly pigly one with another'.

Too higgledy-piggledy, perhaps: many continued to fear the holiday seduced the population 'to Drunkenness, Gluttony, & unlawful Gaming, Wantonness, Uncleanness, Lasciviousness, Cursing, Swearing' and, ultimately, 'all to idleness'. The playwright William Davenant, sometimes said to be Shakespeare's godson, had a character claim that more children were 'begot i' the Christmas Holydaies' than at any other time of the year, 'when the Spirit of Mince-Pie Raignes in the blood'.

And yet the splendidly named Ofspring Blackall, both High Church and High Tory, and soon to be the Bishop of Exeter, felt no need to apologize. Christmas, he wrote, was 'the time of the whole year, for good Eating and Drinking'. For it was the sociable aspect of Christmas that was thriving, even as more formal, organized entertainment was going into decline. In 1635, just before the Civil War, in the Inns of Court, one eager bencher had paid £2,000 to be named Lord of Misrule; fifty years on, the Inns' senior members were effectively forced to bribe one of their juniors to take on the role. And while the legend of the open-handed hospitality of the Middle Ages endured – as late as 1777, to be generous was to be 'as free as an open house at Christmas' – even those great families who entertained, if not as promiscuously as many believe, were altering their behaviour. In part this was a reflection of changes in architectural fashion. No longer did the upper classes live in houses with central great halls. Small tenants were now wined and dined in the kitchens, servants' halls, or housekeepers' rooms, or in the butlers' pantries, while the parlour was for blood-kin and social equals and accommodated fewer high-level servants such as land agents and stewards, who had previously eaten with the family.

That is not to say there was less entertainment: civic bodies, guilds, local grandees, those high in the church hierarchy, all gave breakfasts, dinners and ceremonial feasts. But private citizens, the 'true bred Gallant and man of Quality', began to disdain such occasions, instead 'slip[ping] up to *London*' for the entire cycle of days, 'to save charges', that is, the expense of feasting his tenants and dependants.

Now men of quality were spending Christmas very much like the middle classes: small family groups, if that, on Christmas Day. On 25 December 1661, Pepys went to church, then dined alone with his wife before going out for a walk, followed by a 'merry' supper with friends.

It may be that the violent disorders and topsy-turvydom of the Civil War had temporarily suspended the taste for pretend disorder and topsy-turvydom. Some street festivities continued: court records in Scotland reported people out 'gyseing with a false beard', or 'gyseing in womenis habite', with their 'faces blaickit'. But such customs continued to be more prominent in other parts of Europe. The Scandinavian equivalent of the English hobby-horse was the Yule goat, a wooden beast sometimes topped by an actual goat skull, its tail strung with bells, its jaw manipulated by sticks to snap at bystanders as it pranced down the streets. In some regions an ox, ram, fox or bear replaced the goat as the centrepiece, and young single men, elected Christmas bishops or priests, often joined in. Their faces blackened, or wearing collars of hay, the mock-clergymen oversaw 'weddings' and 'communion'. From at least the sixteenth century, star boys, children dressed as the Magi and wearing paper crowns, some with their faces blackened (for Balthazar, in European Christian tradition often said to be Ethiopian), sometimes accompanied by others portraying Herod, or soldiers, or Judas, carried stars of Bethlehem from house to house, singing carols of the Magi's journey or acting out the nativity story. On 26 December, St Stephen's Day, the Yule or Staffans Ride saw young men compete on horseback. It was also a day for anonymous practical jokes, 'signed' by leaving a Staffan, a doll, at the site of each trick. In Switzerland the gift-bringer known as Samichlaus (Swiss-German for Sankt Klaus, that is, Niklaus) took part in house-to-house processions accompanied by masked young men making noise with horns, bells and guns.

In England, outdoor events clustered not around Christmas Day, but around Twelfth Night. Wassailing was a moveable feast, and some took cider to orchards on Twelfth Day, or drank the health of their farm's oxen with a ring-shaped cake hanging over the largest animal's horn:

Fill up your cups, my merry men all:
For here's the best ox in all the stall;
Oh! He is the best ox, of that there's no mistake,
And so let us crown him with the Twelfth-cake.

More common were domestic Twelfth Night celebrations, replacing the older courtly entertainments. The highlight was the Twelfth Night cake, with its bean and pea to select the Twelfth Night king and queen. In the New World, when the French explorer Robert de La Salle was mapping out the Mississippi Basin, he recorded: 'on Twelve-Day we cry'd, *The King Drinks* . . . tho' we had only Water . . .' Herrick described a similar salute with 'joy sops', or cake dipped in wine, and guests who 'drinke / To the base from the brink / A health to the King and the Queene here'. The cake was probably spice or plum (dried fruit) cake, although it was the nineteenth century before a recipe formally named a fruitcake a Twelfth Night cake. The first recipe we know of for a bean cake, in 1620 in Geneva, was a honey and ginger cake, not fruitcake. Pepys recorded celebrating Twelfth Night in five of the ten years his diary covers, always with a cake to mark the day.*

Pepys and his friends were not just electing a Twelfth king or queen. By now, the evening's entertainment had expanded, and tokens in the cake designated a multitude of 'characters', one for each of the party, selected either from popular current plays, or archetypes – a knave, a cuckold, a slut.† As the tokens got bigger, and there were

---

* Pepys owned a copy of *The Gentlewoman's Cabinet Unlocked*, which contained a fruitcake recipe, so his might have been made with nutmeg, cloves, mace, cinnamon, ginger, sack and rose-water.

† In the seventeenth century a slut was a dirty woman, not a

more of them, while the cakes became more elaborate and
expensive, the names of the characters began to be written
on slips of paper and drawn from a hat instead of being
baked into the cake. Soon pastrycooks stocked cards
printed with an engraving of each character, and street-
sellers sold broadsides printed with Twelfth Night poems,
surrounded by the characters, which could be cut up, one
character to a slip, for the hat.

By the seventeenth century, Christmas was a season. A
book describing 'every action . . . proper to each particular
Moneth' of the year called January, not December, the
month of Christmas:

> it shares the chearfull carrolls of the wassell cup,
> Beasts, Fowls, and Fish come to a generall Execution
> [to be eaten] . . . and Cards and Dice purge many a
> purse . . . a good fire heats all the house, and a full
> Alms-basket sets the beggar to his prayers, Masking,
> and Mumming, and choosing King and Queen, the
> meeting of the friendly, and the mirth of the honest.

Domesticity, warmth, family feeling, carols, eating and
drinking – Christmas was on the move again.

---

sexually promiscuous one, or a servant (given coal fires and lack of
running water, servants were often very dirty). The word could also
have an affectionate overtone: Pepys referred to one of his maids as
'a most admirable Slut [who] pleases [him and his wife] mightily'.

Chapter Four

The ban on Christmas in the British Isles and Puritan New England had, counter-intuitively, made the holiday more, rather than less, visible. However the hospitality of the landed gentry had been organized, it had taken place in their houses: the tenants, their dependants, were welcomed and given food and drink, if only on the doorstep as they wassailed the house.

In the southern American colonies, where the upper classes prided themselves on following English customs, grandees like the planter William Byrd II continued this older, private tradition: he and his family went to church, ate roast beef and turkey and 'In the evening we were merry with nonsense and so were my servants.' Others maintained an air of patrician ignorance of the people's celebrations: Jefferson rarely mentions the day, Washington spent it foxhunting, or doing end-of-year accounts. Some, like Landon Carter, a Virginia planter, found satisfaction 'in not letting my People keep any part of Christmas, because the more civilized show themselves too foolish'. Over thirty years, he mentions Christmas just thirteen times in his diary, mostly in the form of date references – his tobacco would be planted by Christmas, for example.

For the people, however, the day was spent in taverns

and inns, and then out on the streets. For them, Christmas had become a winter carnival. Preachers, of course, disapproved. The Puritan minister Increase Mather saw the holidays – 'as they are called', he added, holding the word out with metaphorical tongs – being spent in drinking, gambling, 'Revellings', 'mad Mirth', and, in case his listeners hadn't been paying attention, he repeated drinking. Yet three of his socially prominent congregants disagreed: 'I Con, they Pro,' Mather noted succinctly. Half a century later there was a significant shift when his son, Cotton Mather, one of the most influential ministers in New England, denounced behaviour arising from the holiday, but not the holiday itself: his 'Black List' condemned the 'Evil Customes' he saw around him. Gambling and drinking that became 'riot' were prevalent at all gatherings, where young people might be tempted. And temptation was notably seasonal: the illegitimate birth rate had a suspicious leap in September and October, more than hinting at what had occurred the previous Christmas.

Even those who were not moralistic saw December more generally as a 'month . . . [where] 'twill rain such a store of sack', as one almanac promised in 1682; in 1714, another defined it as the month of

> Strong-Beer Stout Syder and a good fire
> Are things this season doth require.
> Now some with feasts do crown the day,
> Whilst others loose their coyn in play.

But there was far more to the New World than Puritan New England. Even there, increased immigration had diluted Puritan dominance. In New York, Pennsylvania and down into the Carolinas, Georgia and Virginia,

German and Swiss immigrants arrived with their own traditions; Scottish and Irish immigrants flooded into Pennsylvania, New Jersey and then south and west over the course of the eighteenth century; more immigrants from England attended the mainstream Church of England. Even a small number of new voices could potentially have a significant impact: early eighteenth-century New Amsterdam had a population of about 500 people, who between them spoke eighteen languages.

Christmas therefore became a day that was hard to ignore, no matter how much an individual might desire to. The diary of Elizabeth Drinker, a Philadelphia Quaker, covers nearly half a century, and traces a pattern of gradual acceptance that was not unusual. Quakers did not celebrate the holiday, and in the 1760s and 1770s Drinker generally stayed at home on the 25th. In the 1780s she comments on the holiday activities of others. By 1793 she is still hesitant, calling it 'Christmass, so call'd', but the following year the distancing mechanism is absent, and it has just become 'Christmass day'. By 1797 she had visitors on Christmas Eve; four years later there was a family dinner, and visitors afterwards – the festival had quietly crept up on her.

In 1773 Philip Fithian, a northern, Presbyterian theological student, was employed as a tutor to the children of Landon Carter, the Virginia planter who had himself ignored the day. Presbyterians also shunned Christmas, and one can virtually see Fithian's eyebrows rising as he recorded the pastimes and games of Carter's friends, neighbours and even his own household. By the week before Christmas, he was shocked to find, no one spoke of anything but 'the *Balls*, the *Fox-hunts*, the fine *entertainments*'.

School broke up with a ceremony of 'barring out' the schoolmaster. This was a children's form of topsy-turvy in which they locked the schoolroom door – barred it – against their teacher, forcing him to declare a holiday. The custom had been recorded in England in the sixteenth century, frequently in connection with the election of boy bishops. In 1702, in Williamsburg, Virginia, some boys barricaded themselves inside their schoolroom, but when their schoolmaster and two servants attempted to enter, the boys responded with pistol-fire. This was the first recorded episode of the tradition in the colonies, and the violence may have been the consequence of the participants not being sure of the rules.*

Fithian was also surprised by the guns fired all around the neighbourhood on Christmas Eve, and again on Christmas morning. Firing rounds was traditional in many cultures. In New France, it had been assimilated into religious services: in Quebec, midnight mass was accompanied by cannon-fire. In most places, however, shooting was not formalized, but simply a matter of young men letting off steam. In several parts of Switzerland horns, bells and pistols abounded in the Samichlaus processions on St Nicholas's Day; in one canton, each 5 December saw boys running through their villages with bells and guns, to chase the saint. In Sweden Christmas was 'shot in' – men crept up on their neighbours' houses and fired off guns before racing away unseen and unidentified. Many Swiss, Scandinavian

---

* This was not solely a seasonal tradition. Horace Greeley, later editor of the *New York Tribune*, remembered that in his New Hampshire childhood in the 1820s, it occurred 'On the first of January, and perhaps on some other day that the big boys chose to consider or make a holiday.'

and German-speaking immigrants brought these customs from their native lands, and shooting at Christmas was found in Texas, in the Midwest and in Pennsylvania, as well as across the South.

In England, too, young men in 'antic attire' danced 'with swords or spears' for money, with 'gratitude expressed by firing a gun'. But shooting was rare there. Instead, across the British Isles, as well as dancing, increasingly through the eighteenth century, seasonal plays were performed. These were quite different from the mystery plays of the Middle Ages. Although the plays varied, some elements were consistent everywhere: a hero, often St George, fights a soldier, a devil or a 'Saracen'; one dies, to be miraculously resurrected by a doctor. Secondary characters included a fool, the doctor's assistant, a man carrying a club or a pan, often named Beelzebub, a sweeper and a money-collector. There was also a sword dance, the dancers accompanied by a fool and a Betty, a man dressed as a woman, which might also end in death and resurrection.* The characters were outsiders – devils, soldiers, quack doctors – and as with the Roman Saturnalia, the plays were a way for the working people to demonstrate, in one single, carefully discrete period of time, disrespect for their social superiors. And, like the boy bishops, the plays simulated social upheaval while leaving the status quo unharmed.

The most important thing about any of these popular traditions was that all the participants knew the rules.

---

* Early twentieth-century folklorists situated the origins of these plays in Greek antiquity, or the Roman occupation, or pagan days. However, the first surviving reference to a play with the characters of St George, the Turk and a doctor, dates from 1685; the first surviving play-text itself, half a century after that.

When the rules were understood, it was mumming, or wassailing; otherwise, when one side failed to recognize what was occurring, it could look very much like breaking and entering, or robbery with menaces. In the colonies, the numerous immigrant backgrounds of the residents meant that mutual incomprehension was not unknown. In Salem in 1679, four young men 'invaded' a house, singing and demanding perry, or pear cider, which suggests they might have come from the west of England, known for both its perry-production and mumming. The householder presumably originated elsewhere, for he forced them out, despite their protests that 'it was Christmas Day . . . and they came to be merry and to drink perry'. They showed their displeasure at their Christmas revels being cut short by shouting and throwing 'stones, bones, and other things', damaging the daub of the house, knocking down a fence, breaking into an outside cellar and stealing 'five or six pecks of apples'.

A hundred years later, even when mumming was recognized as such, it was looked down upon by the colonies' upper classes, at least in the urban North. The politician Samuel Breck remembered how his wealthy Boston family in the 1770s and early 1780s suffered annually through a visit from 'the lowest blackguards . . . disguised in filthy clothes', who performed what from his description was clearly a version of the St George hero-play, although just as clearly Breck had never heard of it.

Other immigrant groups practised their own house-to-house traditions. Where districts were sparsely populated, and by immigrants from the same background, this licensed rowdyism was a way of keeping a physically distant population connected. From at least the seventeenth century among the Norwegians of the Upper Midwest, groups of masked, costumed men, with at least one dressed as the Julebukk, wrapped in a goat's skin, and with a horned-head mask, went Julebukking, as in their home country. In southern Pennsylvania, and parts of Virginia, similar Christmas forays were known as belsnickling by the descendants of German immigrants celebrating the arrival of Pelz Nichol, who had become the Belsnickle in Pennsylvania Dutch. Belsnicklers blackened their faces and wore furs or animal skins as they went door-to-door, bringing nuts and cakes for good children, and whips for the bad.*

Where the social structure was oppressive, however, misrule might no longer be a safety valve, but a challenge to the ruling caste, and the American South was, therefore, the site of some of the most intense Christmas events. This might be outright revolt. Possibly because of seasonal licence, as well as the cycle of the agricultural year, slave rebellions often clustered around the holidays. One historian has found records, from the mid-seventeenth century to the early nineteenth century, regarding approximately seventy slave uprisings, both major insurrections and smaller, sporadic outbreaks that might be confined to a single plantation. Of those that can be accurately dated, one in three took place, or was planned to take place, in December.

For those who did not revolt, the season instead brought a permitted form of topsy-turvy, ritualized mumming known as John Canoe, Kuner or Kooner, or Junkanoo,

---

* Note the assimilation in the language, with the addition of the English '-ing' to the Norwegian Julebukk to turn the goat itself into an activity, just as the belsnicklers did with their belsnickling.

which many historians have suggested can be understood as a vehicle of covert social protest that those above could read as mere entertainment, allowing the powerless a single day in the year to speak. The most elaborate form of John Canoeing took place in Jamaica, which had by far the largest colonial slave population. Each region had its own variation, but the formula was for a procession led by John Canoe himself, dressed in a highly decorated mask and carrying a wooden sword, sometimes accompanied by his 'wife', a man in women's clothes, and attended by musicians. They went house to house, dancing and playing in return for cash or alcohol. In the eighteenth century the masks were said to be African; later they could be more fanciful: one engraving shows a John Canoe wearing a model ship on his head, complete with puppet sailors, slaves and slavers. Unusually for this kind of street performance, there were also roles for women. In Jamaica in the eighteenth century, and later in New York, women performed in their own parades, with a Queen at their head.

Consistent across all these forms of Christmas ritual was the gift of food, drink or money. While new year's gifts offered up to the sovereign had vanished, in agricultural areas there was still an expectation that tenants would send their landlords gifts, usually of food from their farms. In 1706 Lady Wentworth complained to her son, the future Earl of Strafford, of her anger 'with al your sneeking tenents; all others send fowls, braun, and severel things, but yours send nothing.' These gifts of obligation to social superiors would disappear in the coming century, even as gifts from social superiors to their inferiors were becoming enshrined as quasi-obligatory, be they gifts from house-holder to shop assistant, master to servant, slave-owner to slave: today we call them tips.

 As Pepys had done in the seventeenth century, a late eighteenth-century Norfolk vicar handed out vails to an astonishing number of recipients: to his tailor's boy, the laundress' maid, the barber's man, a billiard marker, the servants of his friends and servants in inns, a carpenter, 'a woman from the village who came to ask for charity', his coal-merchant, the coal-merchant's servant and his son, the butcher's man, the mason's boy, the chimney sweep and his son, the blacksmith's man, the maltster's man. Some groups' solicitations were formalized. In the British Isles, bellmen called the hour, and often the weather, through the city streets at night ('Past one of the clock, and a cold, frosty, windy morning,' cried a bellman outside Pepys' window in 1660). At Christmas, they had broadsides printed, which headings like 'A Copy of Verses Humbly Presented to all my Worthy Masters and Mistresses in the Parish of —— by —— Bellman and Cryer', followed by verses which might summarize news events from the year, and end with a list of winter cheer for the local householders, and a sign-off: 'when you're safe in bed . . . Think of your Bellman, cold, and void of ease, / Without one comfort, save his hope to please'. The same custom was followed in New England from at least the 1730s by watchmen and news-carriers. There, until the nineteenth century, they were called New Year's notices, and so the custom flourished even in places where Christmas was not habitually observed.

In the American South, slaves and servants used a different method to solicit tips, presented as though it were a game. Whoever shouted 'Christmas gift!' first on Christmas morning won, with the loser obliged to hand over a small gift, or cash. The game was in name only, the slaves always 'winning'. In addition, more routine disbursements were virtually obligatory. A tutor like Philip Fithian was unlikely to have much money, yet during the holidays he paid out to 'the Boy who makes my Fire, [and] blacks my shoes', 'the Fellow who makes the Fire in our School Room', the slave who did his laundry, the woman who made his bed, the barber who shaved and dressed him, the groom who looked after his horse, the boy who waited on him at meals and another who 'calls me to Supper'. And then, in turn, Fithian was tipped by his employer.

It is to be expected that those on the giving, rather than the receiving, end of the transaction found it onerous. Both Christmas tipping, and complaining about tipping, had been constants for more than a hundred years, and would continue to be so for another hundred. On 26 December 1710 the satirist Jonathan Swift groaned, 'By the Lord Harry, I shall be undone . . . with Christmas boxes.'* Others did not merely complain, but attempted to eradicate the custom. In 1767 a group of London bakers placed advertisements stating that they would not be giving Christmas boxes to their customers' servants. Others quickly joined in, and by the end of the century, there were dozens of this type of advertisement placed by guilds and

---

* The origins of the term Boxing Day in Britain to mean 26 December is unclear. The *Oxford English Dictionary*'s first example of usage of the term dates from 1833, but Swift's complaint on the day more than a century earlier suggests otherwise. And in 1743 a witness at a trial felt no need to explain what she meant when she said she had seen a man attacked 'the day after boxing day'.

tradesmen, both forbidding the solicitation of tips by their employees, and announcing their own non-payment.

The bakers' rationale for their refusal was that, if the 'lower ranks' 'wallow[ed] in wealth during the Holydays', as they put it, they would spend it all on alcohol. The association of drinking and Christmas was not confined to aggrieved employers but was typically made by the upper classes when considering those lower down the social scale, both in Britain and in the colonies. One Boston newspaper in 1735 took for granted that men would 'keep drunk all the Christmas Holy-days', given the opportunity. British newspapers agreed. To celebrate Christmas, said one newspaper, was to celebrate 'Rioting and Drunkenness'. This was probably not far from reality. In 1772 Joseph Banks, the naturalist on Captain Cook's first voyage, recorded that the *Endeavour*'s crew kept Christmas 'in the old fashioned way': 'all hands were as Drunk as our forefathers usd to be upon the like occasion'.

Back home, many matched Cook's sailors for seasonal drunkenness. In Aberdeen at Christmas 1784, 'A riotous assemblage . . . stimulated by drink and madness' actually attacked a Roman Catholic church. A few years later, a London court heard from a man who could not say where he had been when his wife was murdered, because 'he had not the smallest recollection of what passed on Christmas Day, he was so much in liquor'. More commonplace was the man brought up on a drunk and disorderly charge in 1831. In his defence, he begged, 'as it was Christmas time, the magistrates would forgive him'. The magistrate was unimpressed: 'every person brought before him during the last three days had made nearly a similar defence, and appeared to think they had a right to commit all manner of excesses with impunity at this festive season'. (Verdict: guilty as charged.)

Even the militantly sober accepted that holiday drinking was inevitable. A fur-trader in northern Ontario, near Hudson Bay, himself 'Spent the Day in Religious Exercise', although 'to prevent hard Drinking' by the other trappers, he read them 'a dissuasive from the Sin of Drunkenness [and then] gave them a Little Liquor'. In other words, he read his men a lecture on the evils of alcohol, and followed it up by serving – alcohol.

As one verse of 'Yankee Doodle' has it,

> Christmas is a-coming Boys,
> We'll go to Mother Chase's,
> And there we'll get a sugar dram
> Sweetened with Melasses.

Alcohol was simply part of Christmas. Yet there were nevertheless changing expectations about how, and where, it should be consumed. In 1754 the *London Magazine* defined Christmas as a festival 'held sacred by good eating and drinking'. The magazine's readers were not drunken sailors, nor young men on the razzle, but gentry and the comfortable middle classes.

They, or so they believed, should be in charge of the holiday. In great part this was owing to the upheavals of the seventeenth century, and the subsequent outpourings of pamphlets worried that now, in the eighteenth, Christmas was no longer what it had once been. The new nostalgia drew comparisons to the good old days, which could turn reality on its head in startling ways.

For example, as we have seen, gambling had long been a pastime of the Christmas holiday. From Henry VIII's reign until 1772, a ritual enabled courtiers to gamble with the monarch himself. On Twelfth Night, it was formally pronounced, 'His Majesty is out', and the king became a mere player, on equal terms with his courtiers. When the evening was concluded, the announcement, 'His Majesty is at home', returned him to pre-eminence. Thousands of pounds, the value of a large country estate, were frequently wagered. But in the eighteenth century, nostalgic reimaginings of these festive indulgences turned wild profligacy into tame domesticity: in 1785 a play praised the days 'When Bess was England's Queen', and cards were played only at Christmas, and then 'for little and their games were few'.

In a similar fashion, what actually took place in people's houses was very different from what was said to have taken place. The *Spectator* magazine, for its prosperous middle-class readers, created the fictional Sir Roger de Coverley, a country squire of the sort that ought to have existed, who at Christmas kept open house 'after the laudable custom of his ancestors', ensuring that the poor had meat, mince pies and beer throughout the twelve days.*

When contrasted with the Christmas customs of two real men in the same century, however, there is little, if anything, that can be recognized. Horace Walpole was of the upper class, the son of Sir Robert Walpole, the prime minister of Britain. He was himself a politician, but is today more famous for popularizing the new Gothic style, both at Strawberry Hill, his house in south-west London,

---

* Sir Roger was given the name of a popular dance of the previous century. Various versions, to various tunes, can be seen on YouTube.

and in his novel *The Castle of Otranto*. Of greater importance to social historians are his letters, which fill forty-eight large volumes. And there his passing references to the holiday over four decades show upper-class views of the day to be strongly at odds with Sir Roger de Coverley's report. In 1743 Walpole described some friends as being 'a thousand times more agreeable than Christmas, which, since I have done loving mince pies, I have never admired at all'. Five years later, he reiterated his distaste: 'I have stuck no laurel and holly in my windows, I eat no turkey . . . I have no tenants to invite . . .' And in 1788 he mockingly expressed admiration for those who adhered to traditions such as 'making one's neighbours and all their servants drunk'.

James Woodforde, a generation younger, was a Norfolk vicar who recorded his daily doings for more than forty years in a diary that almost matches Walpole's letters in extent. Unlike Walpole, Woodforde was a man of merely comfortable means, rather than of wealth. His income assured him a place in the upper middle classes, but his interests were entirely rural: he hunted, he visited the local squire and nearby clergymen. Rarely moving outside this limited ambit, he observed many of the Christmas customs Walpole disdained. Singers called at his vicarage annually, as had mummers in his youth in the West Country, although not after he moved to Norfolk in 1774. There were also the men who rang the church bells year round, who came to the vicarage for their seasonal handout, sometimes in cash, sometimes alcohol. From 1778 he was also visited by a man 'with his 10. Bells [who] . . . played before my Company'. These bells were 'of his own Construction', not a traditional practice, but he gave 'us his annual Musick' every Christmas, for which he received 1s. 6d., and 'Victuals &

Drink'. Occasionally a single indigent individual, such as 'a poor old singing Man', also received sixpence.

Meanwhile, Woodforde and his family and friends enjoyed parties and dinners over the twelve days, without laying any particular emphasis on Christmas Day itself. One year his niece Nancy, who kept house for him, went to Norwich, neither she nor Woodford seeming to be concerned that this left him alone on Christmas Day. He also recorded attending 'Christmas dinner' on 29 December. In his younger days, Woodforde went to parties around Twelfth Night or New Year, including one 'where I spent the whole night and part of the morning till 4 o'clock a dancing'. However, that was a celebration for the local apothecary, who was coming out of his apprenticeship. On 11 January one year Woodforde sighed, 'I am heartily weary of visiting so much as I have,' but as a clergyman, 'if I did not it would be taken amiss'. Other years he celebrated hard: 'We were exceeding merry indeed all the Night', playing cards until six in the morning, then 'serenad[ing] the Folks that were a bed with our best on the Hautboy [an ancestor of the oboe]'.

What Woodforde did observe, with great regularity, was St Thomas's Day, 21 December. 'Gooding', sometimes called mumping, or 'going a-corning', when seasonal charity was begged from local households, went back to the sixteenth century. It was the eighteenth century, however, before it centred on St Thomas's Day, when it also became going 'a-Thomassing'.

As open-house hospitality had narrower parameters than nostalgia would admit, so too did gooding. Throughout his four decades in Norfolk, Woodforde routinely gave sixpence each to the poor of his parish. But it was very specifically of *his* parish: 'I had at my House fifty five, gave only to 53 – the other two not living in the Parish.' It is also notable that when he began his charitable donations in 1764, each recipient got sixpence; thirty-six years later he was still giving sixpence, regardless of the economic hardships brought by the French wars: 'Wheat very dear indeed', 'Flour very difficult to get at all'. In another seasonal custom, Woodforde gave six or seven men a 'very fine Surloin of Beef rosted' and 'Plumb Puddings' in his kitchen every 25 December. His clerk usually attended; otherwise the men (they were almost always men) tended to be the oldest in the parish. Occasionally a woman was included – once it was a maid who had worked for him for years; sometimes he sent 'a dinner' or, in later years, a shilling, home to the wives of the men in the kitchen.

Other, more institutional, versions of this type of Christmas charity were becoming more common. Sunday schools and other organizations held mass dinners for those who might otherwise go without. One Sunday school served 350 dinners on Boxing Day, when, in a rare instance of surviving topsy-turvy, 'The benefactors' served the working classes.* The meal that was served up was not recorded, but it is likely that it was the same as Woodforde gave his 'poor old men': roast beef and plum pudding. In his early days as a young curate in Somerset, Woodforde had eaten the same for his own Christmas dinner, but at

---

* It was possibly an unthinking recognition of the holiday's topsy-turvy traditions that led Jane Austen to have the upstart, socially ambitious Mr Elton propose to the landed, upper-class Emma on Christmas Eve. Emma's rejection of his suit makes clear social class is key: 'She was insulted . . . he was her inferior.' The novel was published on 23 December 1815.

Oxford in the 1770s, his Christmas Day dining in hall became more elaborate: 'two fine Codds boiled with Fryed Soals round them & Oyster Sauce, a fine Surloin of Beef rosted, some Peas Soup & an Orange Pudding for the first Cours, for the Second we had a Lease of Wild Ducks rosted, a fore-Q[r]. of Lamb & Sallad & Mince Pies . . . After . . . there was a fine Plumb Cake . . .'* Once he had moved to East Anglia, plum cake made no further appearances on his holiday table, although, living as he did in the region of English turkey-rearing, 'a fine rost Turkey' often did, and not only at Christmas.

By now, the components of the Christmas meal that are still served in the twenty-first century were falling into place. In 1747, Hannah Glasse's *The Art of Cookery, Made Plain and Easy*, considered by many to be the first cookery book in English for the home cook, included relatively little that was specific to Christmas, and of that little, did not group it as holiday cooking. The pudding section contained a recipe for plum pudding, but with no mention of Christmas; there was a recipe for mince pies, which also made no reference to the holiday; and a recipe for Yorkshire Christmas pies, which did, because 'These Pies are often sent to *London* in a Box as presents; therefore the Walls [the pastry] must be well built.' Under 'soops', the housewife could learn 'To make Plumb-Porridge for Christmas': thicken beef stock with bread, strain it and boil it down, adding currants, raisins, prunes, mace, cloves, nutmeg, sugar, salt, sack, claret and lemon-juice.

---

* Until the 1860s the fashion in dining in Britain was not too far from the 'messes' of the Middle Ages, although the array of mixed sweet and savoury courses was now called 'removes'. Diners selected from among them, and no one was expected to eat everything.

Robert Seymour, 'The Norfolk Stage at Christmas', from
Thomas Hervey's *The Book of Christmas* (1836).

Barely forty years later, however, plum porridge was
'old-fashioned', sneered *The Times*, and 'discarded from
every family in the kingdom except for the Royal family'.
Christmas pies, filled with fowl and game, survived, as
Hannah Glasse had written, frequently sent from the country as a gift to city friends. Turkeys too were traditionally
sent from the country, so much so that they were the subject of jokes: 'Upwards of 30,000 Turkeys fell martyrs' to
the day, reported *The Times* in heavy-handed jest, and
engravings of laden stagecoaches from Norfolk provided
visual corroboration.[*]

[*] Turkeys did not travel well. Before the railways in the nineteenth century, almost all animals were driven alive to market and
slaughtered there. Turkeys however, had to be fitted with little

Holiday specialities, by the eighteenth century, still included Twelfth cakes, now mostly bought from pastry-cooks. These were for the rich, however, and references to them are almost entirely from London. We know less about the cakes of the middle classes, or those outside London – if indeed those outside London did celebrate Twelfth Night with any regularity.

For it is possible that Twelfth Night was a London custom, one observed mainly by the fashionable and aristo-cratic; a custom that, simply because of the way history has primarily been drawn from the behaviour and records of the ruling classes, has been assumed by historians to have been marked by everyone, across the country. In London, certainly, it was an important day. Pastrycooks' cards and broadsides were widely available. If Isaac Cruikshank's print 'Old Square Toes was Cuckold' reflected reality, the evening might play to the more louche side of the holiday, depicting as it did a young woman pretending to draw her character from a hat held by a handsome young man, while he instead slips her a note from himself.

Cakes being expensive, even in London, the less-well-off may have participated only by admiring, as the highly elaborate confections were placed in pastrycooks' windows to enthral passers-by. Others amused themselves in less

---

leather boots to protect their feet on their march, and the expedi-tion began in August: they lost so much weight en route that the fattening-up process had to recommence once they reached their destination. The expense of the boots, and of the prolonged walk and feeding, ensured an extraordinarily high price for them once they finally were put on sale. At Christmas, however, the birds were killed where they were reared, Norfolk being a mere three days' journey from London by stagecoach.

Robert Seymour, 'Twelfth Night in the London Streets', from
Thomas Hervey's *The Book of Christmas* (1836).

acceptable ways, like the boys who indulged in the Twelfth
Night practice of 'nailing': they mingled with the crowds
outside the pastrycooks in order to surreptitiously tack the
coat-tails of unsuspecting men to an adjacent wall, or even
pin them to the skirts of a nearby, equally unaware, woman.

Outside London, and the habits of aristocratic landed
families, many allowed Twelfth Night to pass them by. The
first English recipe to refer to a rich fruitcake as a Twelfth
cake was published only in 1768, and says carefully: 'This
is called a *twelfth cake* at *London.*' There is little evidence to
suggest the day was celebrated outside the capital, and by
anyone other than the gentry classes. Parson Woodforde
attended many parties on 5 January in Norfolk, but never
called them Twelfth Night celebrations. As he entertained

and was entertained year-round, there is no certainty that day meant anything to him. In the British Library's collection of more than 200 local and national newspapers, there are a mere handful of references to Twelfth Night that do not in some way relate to London.*

Yet such was the dominance of the capital that the customs associated there with the night gave rise to more than one figure of speech. As early as the sixteenth century, Tudor historian Polydore Virgil had recognized Twelfth Night's disquieting inversion, when 'all the household and family . . . must be obedient' to one who was normally their social inferior. And so the Twelfth Night King or Queen became a synonym for falsity. Lady Jane Grey was dismissed as 'nothing but a Twelfth-day Queen' in the sixteenth century; a century later, Philip IV of Spain contemptuously labelled the Portuguese usurper 'a king of the bean'. As the cakes became more elaborate, and sugar less expensive, the powdered sugar that dusted the cakes became a metaphor for grey hair, and thus age. A sermon on the revolutionary times in the 1770s refers to men 'with their *curled pates* (frosted o'er like a *twelfth-cake*)'.

 That was published first in Britain, and exported to Philadelphia, where it was nothing but a phrase. In the colonial South, however, where the upper classes liked to claim close kinship to upper-class England, Twelfth Night was a great event. Planters from William Byrd in 1740 to

---

* What might today be the last gasp of this holiday was established in 1794, with the death of Robert Baddeley, who had been a cook, then a valet, before becoming an actor at Drury Lane. In his will he left money for an annual Twelfth cake for that theatre's company, which continues to be served there every 5 January, although it has been renamed the Baddeley cake in his honour.

Landon Carter in the 1770s held parties with Twelfth cakes. In Virginia, in 1775, among one group of friends at least, whomever was crowned king one year hosted the next year's party, while that year's queen had 'the trouble of making the cake'.

The holidays might not have been thought of as 'trouble', but they were definitely becoming more elaborate.

Chapter Five

As the eighteenth century progressed, new customs were established, especially among the middle classes, who were gradually transforming the holiday. In part this was owing to the spread of antiquarianism – the now fashionable enthusiasm for recording observations on the artefacts and customs of the people, which gave new life to many traditions previously practised only by the rural or the working-classes. As early as Pepys's day, immediately fol-lowing the Restoration of Charles II, and the return of Christmas after the Puritan interregnum, churches had returned to tradition, and were decorated with greenery again, Pepys finding his pew on 23 December 1660 'all covered with Rosemary and baize [bay]'. (As ever, not everyone approved. One congregant complained that his church had so much greenery heaped around the pulpit that it was like hearing 'the Word out of a Bush, like Moses'.)

As the poet Herrick had recorded, mistletoe had been part of the holiday from the seventeenth century, although the tradition of kissing underneath it appeared only in the early nineteenth century, for reasons that remain unknown. By that time, antiquarians had read their Roman history. Pliny had written that the Druids in Gaul – that is, France – had ceremonially harvested mistletoe when they found it growing on oak trees, which they revered. This was somehow reinterpreted to say that these ceremonies had been held in Britain too, and at Christmas, although Pliny had made no mention of either the country or the season. Despite that, it created a new custom with an 'ancient' history.

In a similar fashion, in 1777 the antiquarian John Brand told his readers that 'Our Fore-Fathers' had customarily lit large candles on Christmas Eve. Certainly it had been recorded in 1633, at least proverbially, by the poet Francis Quarles, who compared a hypocrite to 'a Christmas Candle, whose good name / Crowns his faire actions with a glorious *flame* . . . but . . . stinks at going out'. But between that date and Brand's book lie nearly 150 years in which there is no surviving reference to the custom. Had it continued, and simply gone unmentioned in literature, diaries and letters? Or did Brand's book revive a practice that had long been dead? Or perhaps his book gave life to what had previously been no more than a poetic metaphor? We cannot know, but by 1785, eight years after Brand's book was published, Parson Woodforde was writing, 'My large Wax Candle was lighted up this Evening for an Hour, being Christmas Day,' as though it were an annual event, although in his previous quarter-century of diary-keeping he had never once mentioned it. It was another five years before he wrote of it again, and then he continued to do so until 1799, after which it vanished once more. Likewise, there were a number of references to the custom in Yorkshire in the nineteenth century and into the twentieth, but whether these were traditions that had been handed down through generations, or were practices newly learned from books, there is no way of knowing.

Other customs flowered more abundantly in the eighteenth century. In the fifteenth and sixteenth centuries, as reports of trees blossoming on Christmas Eve had become current in Germany, so had the tale of Joseph of Arimathea in England. In this local legend, Joseph of Arimathea, who in the Gospels gives his own tomb to be Christ's resting place, was said to have travelled to Glastonbury with the Holy Grail; after his death there, a tree grew by his tomb 'that on the 24 of December would be bare and naked . . . on the next day being Christmas Day, it would be full of blossoms, and flourishing . . .' Sadly, the story concluded, it had been chopped down 'by ignorant zeal in the late times of Rebellion'. Eighteenth-century tourism thus lacked a drawing-card, and so soon the tree, now usually a hawthorn, was reinstated, still annually flowering, as were many cuttings across the country that were said to have been taken from it. In 1752, when the change from the Julian to the Gregorian calendar meant that eleven days were lost, perhaps as many as two thousand people gathered in front of a hawthorn in Buckinghamshire, to see if it blossomed. (It didn't.)* By the 1770s the Glastonbury thorn was legendary, and Horace Walpole's 'Glastonbury thorns [who] bloom at their Christmas' is a whimsical way of referring to those who were still flourishing in the winter of their lives.

---

* The Julian calendar gained nearly three days every 400 years, an anomaly corrected with the introduction of the Gregorian calendar, first in 1582 in the territories ruled by Spain. Other Catholic countries followed, but Protestant Europe took longer. Britain adopted the new dating in 1752, when the day after 2 September became 14 September. (It is, incidentally, for this reason that the British tax year ends on 5 April, which under the old calendar was Lady Day, 25 March and New Year's Day.)

By the beginning of the eighteenth century, greenery more generally, being so routine at Christmas, itself came to be called, simply, 'Christmas'.* Kissing boughs arrived slightly later in the century, in the south and west, and were a rural, working-class decoration. These consisted of whatever greenery was available, or inexpensive. Measuring up to a metre and a half across, they were made of two to four crossed hoops of greenery decorated with apples and oranges, 'bits of coloured ribbons and paper roses', and other 'various brightly coloured ornaments'. For the more prosperous, greenery on its own was sufficient. Parson Woodforde purchased holly every Christmas Eve to decorate the windows in his parlour, as well as more for his servants in the kitchen.

Branches and the odd holly berry paled in comparison to the type of Christmas greenery that was seen across the German-speaking lands. Since that first decorated indoor Christmas tree in a private house in Strasbourg in 1605, the custom had continued to gain ground. Indoor, decorated, candle-lit trees appeared first in upper-class urban Protestant homes, and moved down the social scale and into rural areas as the century progressed. The names for the tree reflected religious allegiance. To Protestants the tree was a *Weihnachtsbaum*, or *Tannenbaum*, a Christmas or fir tree; Protestantism became 'the *Tannenbaum* religion', and the trees were sometimes *Lutherbäume*, [Martin] Luther trees. Where Catholic regions adopted the tree, it became a *Christbaum*, a *Lichterbaum*, or *Lebensbaum*, a tree of Christ,

* The *Oxford English Dictionary* gives 1825 for its first citation of 'Christmas' to mean seasonal greenery as decoration, but as early as 1706 a newspaper article used the phrase 'Windows . . . stuck with Christmas' without needing to explain.

light, or life; Württemberg had *Christkindleinsbäume*, Christ child trees. Princess Liselotte von der Pfalz (b. 1652), later to marry the brother of Louis XIV of France, remembered the trees of her German childhood, either in her birthplace of Heidelberg, or in Saxony, where she lived for some years. Each child had their own small boxwood tree placed on a table, around which, 'fixed up like altars', were gifts: 'new clothes, silver, dolls, sugar candy'. By whatever name, and however displayed, by the 1770s and 1780s, trees were an integral part of the German Christmas, whether a small tree in a pot placed on a table, a fir-tree tip hanging point downwards from the ceiling, a tree, point upwards, with the end sharpened and spearing an apple, or, among Pietist or evangelical communities, branches decorated with candles and sweets placed on wooden pyramid frames.

This German tradition travelled to England in the final quarter of the eighteenth century. Goethe's novel *The Sorrows of Young Werther* was a sensational popular success in German in 1774, and was translated into English in the 1780s, including its description of a candle-lit Christmas tree decorated with sweets and apples. In 1789 the husband of a lady-in-waiting to Queen Charlotte, the German wife of George III, suggested putting up 'an illuminated tree, according to the German fashion', but she was doubtful – 'I thought our children too young to be amused at so much expense and trouble', and besides, she demurred, all their friends were away. It sounds as though she and her husband had seen such trees, although it was only in 1800, at Windsor, that Queen Charlotte erected the first tree that can be firmly dated in Britain. (This might not qualify as a tree in modern terms, however, sounding more like English greenery: a branch 'fixed on a board'.)

What is as interesting is the phrase that followed that description: 'and under it was a neat model of a farmhouse surrounded by figures of animals'. The Moravian Brethren were one of the oldest Protestant denominations, dating from the fifteenth century. By the 1730s the Moravians were at the forefront of the Protestant missionary movement, including, in 1741, travelling to the newly christened Bethlehem in Pennsylvania and, not long after, to North Carolina. These Moravian communities, and their Central European heritage, were an important source of Christmas traditions in the New World. The Brethren in Bethlehem in the middle of the eighteenth century erected 'several small pyramids and one large pyramid of green brushwood', laden with candles, apples and 'pretty verses'. And, as with Queen Charlotte, the description continued: 'Close by were to be seen the Bethlehem stables, with the oxen and the asses, as also, the shepherds.'

The nativity scene, or *crèche*, or *presepio*, or *Krippe*, had been a feature of Christmas in Catholic countries since Francis of Assisi was said to have created one in 1223. His was a 'living' scene, where real people and animals posed against the background of a cave to replicate the story of the nativity, but inanimate models, made of wood, clay, paper, or other materials, quickly became more common. By the fourteenth and fifteenth centuries nativity scenes were seen across northern Italy, from the Tyrol down to Modena.

The Jesuits created the first one recorded north of the Danube, in Prague in the later sixteenth century. Three areas of Germany became particularly famous for *Krippen*: Bavaria, Saxony and Silesia, the latter also being one of the main embarkation-points for many of the Moravian

Brethren who travelled to Pennsylvania. And, like the Catholic communities they had been surrounded by in the Old World, the Moravians had a strong cult of the infant Jesus, which, together with nativity scenes, went with them to the New. There they were transformed into 'Putzes'.

Putzen in German means to clean or to polish, but in sixteenth-century Saxon dialect it also meant to decorate, especially churches, although not solely at Christmas. In Pennsylvania, Putz became the word for a local form of decorated nativity scene.[*] In the early days, the tree, the pyramid and the Putz were sometimes interchangeable, and today it can be difficult to say exactly what was on display, as when one Pennsylvania diarist recorded in 1818: 'This afternoon Herman took apart and put away his beautiful pyramidal Christmas Putz'.

The Moravians, coming from post-Reformation Germany at a time when the carol genre was flourishing there, may also have brought Christmas carols with them. In England, too, by this period, carols were slowly re-emerging from their enforced Puritan sleep. In 1694 the poet laureate, Nahum Tate, had published *A New Version of the Psalms of David, Fitted to the Tunes used in Churches*, which included his most famous work, the lyrics of 'While Shepherds Watched Their Flocks by Night'. While not everyone approved of what was considered to be a shocking lack of gravity in the lyrics, the carol was widely popular.[†] Soon English carols

---

[*] While the word is capitalized, as all German nouns are, the plural has an English ending, Putzes, following the pattern of the belsnickles and Julebukks.

[†] One generation's populism is another's high culture. The eighteenth-century antiquary John Brand dismisses a carol from *c*.1548: 'It is hardly credible that such a Composition . . . should

were being written across the religious spectrum: in 1739 the Methodist Charles Wesley wrote the words to 'Hark the Herald Angels Sing' (Mendelssohn's tune, adapted by another Englishman, had to wait another century); the following year, an English Roman Catholic in France produced 'Adeste Fideles' (the English version, 'O Come All Ye Faithful', also appeared in the following century). And in 1742 the London music world was introduced to what has now become a Christmas favourite, Handel's *Messiah*, but which was then usually performed at Easter. (Only the first section concerns the nativity; the next two tell the Easter passion story; and the final moves on to universal redemption.)

Outside of London, and the educated classes, carols were even more popular, but they were not new. In Britain, ballads and traditional carols had long circulated in chapbooks, broadsides and other cheap publications of the working classes, but they were only now receiving middle-class attention. 'The Holly and the Ivy' provides a prime example of the difficulties of pinning these popular ballads down to a specific time or place. Until the words and music were recorded in the early twentieth century, its sole printed source was a broadside dating from 1864, itself claiming to be a reprint of an older broadside dating back 'about one-and-a-half centuries', which places its origins at

---

ever have been thought serious,' he grieves. Had its author *'designed to have rendered his Subject ridiculous, he could not more effectu- ally have made it so.'* The lyrics he cites – 'O my dear heart, young Jesu sweet, / Prepare a cradle in thy spreit' – indicate that this is 'Balulalow', a sixteenth-century Scottish lullaby later refashioned by Benjamin Britten in his *Ceremony of Carols* (1942), one of his greatest, and most widely performed, works.

the beginning of the eighteenth century, making it very early. We have no evidence that that earlier printing was the first, however, and the carol might therefore be even older. The refrain, 'The rising of the sun, / And the running of the deer, / The playing of the merry organ, / Sweet singing in the choir', makes no sense, and one modern scholar has dismissed it as 'Olde Englishe trumpery that a canny broadside publisher of 1710 might have strung together.' But our information comes entirely from that 1864 broadside. Was there really an earlier broadside, and if so, was the printer correct in thinking it to be 150 years old? It might have been more recent; it might have been older. Or, of course, there might have been no earlier broadside at all, and the 1864 printer might have invented it to give his own innovation an air of legitimacy.

As in Britain, so too in the colonies. Although carols were becoming popular in Catholic Latin America at this time, in the first half of the eighteenth century, religious 'tune books' in Protestant New England included no holiday music until 1750, when one Boston tune book included an English hymn based on the nativity story. Another half dozen or so followed in the next decade, and by 1770 many colonial clergy and church organists were producing Christmas songs of their own. In the slave states, Christmas music was developing independently among the black populations, with spirituals like 'A-Rockin' All Night' and 'The Angel Band' possibly dating to the eighteenth century (although they might be somewhat later). By the end of the century, seasonal spirituals were widely sung in the United States.

Spirituals were typically more concerned with the nativity – with the spiritual, indeed – than the carols of the local white populations, which, as in Britain, focused on food and drink, especially the items that had become, if not available to all, an ideal that all hoped for – turkey, plum pudding and mince pies. Several of the more successful British cookbooks of the century were printed in Virginia from the 1740s onwards, and thus their traditional holiday eating pattern became assimilated in the American South. The North followed the same path. In 1786 in New York, despite her Quaker upbringing, the wife of the Secretary of the Continental Congress served a Christmas dinner with 'as good mince pies & as fat a turkey as you can procure'.

It was not all imitation: the cultural melting-pot of the new USA also produced many novelties. *American Cookery* was published in 1796 in Connecticut, its author probably from New York state, since she included a recipe for 'A Christmas Cookey', the first time a biscuit was designated as specific to the holiday. The word cookey, or, today, cookie, a sweet biscuit, is from the Dutch *coeckje* (in modern spelling, *koekje*), little cake, and cookies were, in New York City, a New Year's item. John Pintard (1759–1844), a merchant who in the nineteenth century was to have profound influence on the developments of other holiday elements (see pp. 101–4), remembered the custom in his youth: 'New Year was . . . most boisterous & . . . began at Midnight, Drums beating Firing of Guns, huzzas, & [visitors] calling at friendly doors, to congratulate the family & get a New Years dram & cookey.'

In the German communities, too, small gifts were exchanged at year end, as had been traditional in the immigrants' homelands, the items often purchased in the Christmas markets that had been common in Germany since the Middle Ages. The first holiday market in Germany had been held in Cölln (now part of Berlin), and from the mid-fifteenth century had sold honey-cakes, while several Swiss towns had a Chlausmarkt around St Nicholas's Day. Berlin later had a famous *Weihnachtsmarkt* between 12 December and the end of the year. By 1796 its 250 booths sold everything from textiles to toys, gold and silver trinkets, wigs, carved wooden objects, clothes and *Nascherei*, holiday cakes or sweet things more generally; behind these were smaller, humbler stalls offering boots, shoes, baskets, household goods and cheap books.

Books, particularly books for children, were soon expected 'Christmas and New-Year's Gifts' – the two holidays linked together made a standard phrase. In 1789 a Boston publisher translated a French children's book, *L'Ami des enfants* (1782/3), as *The Children's Friend*, with stories detailing the daily life of middle-class children. In '*Les Etrennes*' ('New Year's Day Gifts'), the Parisian children receive New Year's gifts of cake, candied fruit, sweetmeats, toy soldiers, counters for board-games, china figurines, a microscope and a watch. In the Boston edition, the story-title became 'The Christmas-Box', but the gifts remained the same: apparently New England children were comfortable with the idea of these expensive seasonal presents.

Gift-giving, and gift-receiving, were indicative of changes not merely to holiday customs, but to society more generally. Urbanization and industrialization meant that increasing numbers had moved from small, densely interwoven villages and towns to vast cities of strangers, making the immediate family the primary unit of private life. As child mortality declined, parents were able to invest more personalized attention in each individual child, even as the professional and middle classes expanded, allowing the children to stay out of the workforce longer. At the same time, the ideas of thinkers such as John Locke filtered into those same middle classes. Locke, in *Some Thoughts Concerning Education*, suggested that good men and women were made, not born: 'Nine parts of Ten are what they are, Good or Evil, useful of not, by their Education'. Toys therefore became a threefold conduit from parent to child: they were a means of educating young owners with their parents' values; they were expressions of parental love; and their purchase was a symbol of parental success.

Giving toys was also traditional, in that it maintained hierarchical gift-giving practices: the gift was given by a social superior (the parent) to an inferior (the child) in both age and status. Parson Woodforde's presents to his nieces and nephews were little different from the tips he gave the baker's boy: cash, or occasionally ribbons, or on one occasion an almanac, another a green silk gown he had inherited from 'my poor Aunt Parr'. One can similarly imagine poor Aunt Parr, had she not died, handing on the unwanted gown to her maid.

Such gifts from parents, or other relatives, were frequently known too by the same name as servants' tips: Christmas boxes.

> Some Boys are rich by Birth beyond all Wants,
> Beloved by *Uncles*, and kind good old *Aunts*;
> When Time comes round a *Christmas-Box* they bear,
> And one Day makes them *rich* for all the *year*.

But gifts were also increasingly exchanged among friends. On the Lewis and Clark expedition, the first government-sponsored expedition of discovery, covering more than half of the USA as the company trekked from Missouri to Oregon in 1805, Lieutenant Clark 'rcved a present of a Fleeshe Hoserey [fleece hosiery, or stockings] vest draws [a vest and drawers, or long underwear] & Socks of Capt Lewis, pr. Mockerson [a pair of moccasins]' and a basket from his men, and a 'Doz weasels tales . . . & Some black roots' from some of the indigenous people living nearby. In return, the expedition leaders divided up their tobacco between their men as Christmas presents, giving handkerchiefs to those who didn't chew. And while weasels' tails presumably did not feature heavily in many people's Christmas lists, it is noticeable that otherwise the gifts were items of utility: socks, slippers and underwear, which would all become staples of Christmas gift-giving.

Clark and company exchanged their gifts in the new style, on Christmas Day, not at New Year. One of the first advertisements in Britain to promote a Christmas gift was printed in 1728: an anodyne necklace, for a teething baby. By 1743 an anthology of stories, jokes and other light fare was advertised with the subtitle, 'A Christmas-box for gay Gallants and good Companions', and the most common Christmas gift for children became books, including in the 1750s *Nurse Truelove's Christmas-Box or, The Golden Play-Thing for Little Children*, published by the pioneering children's publisher John Newbery. (This one in particular was soon also a staple of advertisements in colonial newspapers.) Nor was the gimmicky, vulgar Christmas publication an invention of the twentieth century: in 1760 and 1761, *The Boghouse Miscellany* was advertised widely (*right*).

After the death of her small son in 1773, the author, society hostess and bluestocking Elizabeth Montagu dismissed Christmas outside of fashionable London as entirely 'for the young'. By the end of the century, advertisers thought so too, and as well as books, a few advertisement for toys began to appear, like 'the Talisman; or, Christmas Conjuror, a new diverting game, in a real Mahogany Box', although at 1s. 6d., it was a toy for the wealthy.

Across the Atlantic, the earliest advertisements were also for books, both educational and religious, such as a 1738 catechism, 'very proper for a New-Year's Gift to Children'. It took another few decades for such advertisements to become common, but by 1770 one New York newspaper had broadened both its audience and gift-giving, promoting jewellery, snuffboxes, toothpick cases, and backgammon and chess sets as 'proper Presents to and from Ladies and Gentlemen at this Season'.

And as gifts were becoming more widespread, it made sense, therefore, that the traditional bringers of gifts should also gain prominence. And that is exactly what happened.

Chapter Six

 By the eighteenth century, personifications of the season were commonplace. The British Isles had variations on Father Christmas, usually an elderly man known for eating and drinking to excess rather than for giving gifts. Elsewhere, however, these figures tended to bring good things with them, and were already more oriented towards children. The Christkind visited in German-speaking lands, although he was unknown in neighbouring countries, and in 1711 Louis XIV's German sister-in-law, Liselotte von der Pfalz, was upbraided for suggesting he be introduced to the French court: 'You want to bring us your German customs to spend more money,' her husband accused. German-speakers also welcomed the visits of St Nicholas and his helpers, as did the Dutch, their home country giving birth to the most famous gift-bringer in the West over the past two centuries, Santa Claus.

Or perhaps not. The standard story of Santa Claus runs as follows. St Nicholas of Myra was bishop of the Lycian Greek town of Myra (now Demre, in Turkey) in the fourth century, although it was *The Golden Legend*, a compilation of the lives of the saints written by a Genoese churchman around 1260, that established most of his story. In that telling, the bishop is said to have tossed three bags of gold through an impoverished nobleman's window to provide dowries for his three daughters so that they would not be sold into prostitution. A later legend told of a wicked innkeeper who murdered, cut up and salted the bodies of three schoolboys, to serve as meat in his inn, a dastardly plot that was foiled by the saint. Elsewhere he was said to have rescued ships from winter storms. Drawing on these themes, St Nicholas over time became the patron saint of sailors, and, particularly, of children. His saint's day, 6 December, became the day on which schoolchildren were rewarded or punished for their year's work, or were given a holiday, and his attributes included sacks, to represent the bags of gold. By the sixteenth century in the Netherlands, on the eve of his saint's day, figures of St Nicholas went from house to house, accompanied by his servant, Zwarte Piet, to catechize the children, rewarding those who had been good with sweets, those who had been bad with switches, or lumps of coal.

And from there, the story continues, Dutch emigrants to New Amsterdam, later Manhattan, took St Nicholas with them, and their version of the saint's name, Sint Nicolaas, was rendered by the city's English-speaking population as Sinterklaas, then corrupted to Santa Claus, to be immortalized in Clement Clarke Moore's 1823 poem, 'A Visit from St Nicholas', better known by its opening lines:

> 'Twas the night before Christmas, when all thro'
>   the house
> Not a creature was stirring, not even a mouse;
> The stockings were hung by the chimney with care,
> In hopes that St Nicholas soon would be there . . .

Except that here we must stop and rewind, for little in

this story actually happened. It is likely that the fourth-century Bishop of Myra never existed: the first mention of him comes two hundred years after he supposedly lived. By the sixteenth century, however, while he visited the Netherlands every December, there are difficulties in getting him from there to North America.

From 1624 New Netherland, the North American Dutch colony, was governed by a treaty with the Dutch Republic, the seven Dutch provinces that had freed themselves from Habsburg domination. And that treaty established the Protestant Reformed Church as the official church of the New World territories – a church that permitted no recognition of saints, nor of saints' days. Furthermore, while the territory was politically and legally Dutch, its inhabitants were as ethnically mixed as those of modern-day New York: of the region's approximately 3,500 residents, as many as 2,000 may have been English, and many more were of German or Scandinavian origin. By the end of the seventeenth century, as little as 2 per cent of the population of the city was actually Dutch.

So, no saints' days, and Dutch traditions most likely practised by no more than a tiny minority. Instead of deriving from folklore, therefore, or quaint colonial customs, or religion, the American emergence of Santa Claus was rooted in late-eighteenth-century politics, in the formation of clubs and societies based around ethnic or cultural groups, which came together to promote themselves and their fellow immigrants: a St Andrew's Society for Scots immigrants, St David's for the Welsh, St Patrick and St George for the Irish and the English. In 1786 a mostly Irish group called itself the Sons of St Tammany. (Tamanend had been a Lenni-Lenape chief when European colonists first established Philadelphia, so the choice of name was a jab at the British.)

One of the founders of the Sons of St Tammany was a merchant named Lewis Pintard (although he was of Huguenot, rather than Irish, descent), the guardian of his orphaned nephew, John Pintard. Pintard Jr also became a merchant, but he was more interested in charitable endeavours and in history than in trade, and in 1804 helped found the New-York Historical Society, which took St Nicholas as its emblem, possibly as a nod to Pintard's Huguenot heritage: many American Huguenots originated in the Low Countries, especially Wallonia, where the cult of Nicholas was particularly prominent. Pintard himself had previously marked the saint's day, 6 December, as a private day of thanksgiving for the world's first three republics: those of France, the United Provinces and the United States.

In this same period, a young writer named Washington Irving was drawing on New York's Dutch history for political satire, contrasting what he thought of as a kinder and gentler Old World in New Amsterdam with the hustle and bustle of modern New York. In his 1809 burlesque, *A History of New-York*, published under the mock-Dutch pseudonym of Diedrich Knickerbocker (and thus often later known as the *Knickerbocker History*), to be a New Amsterdammer rather than a New Englander was to be a *real* New Yorker. The New-York Historical Society members also used New Amsterdam as a contrast to what they viewed as the ills of the present in their rapidly changing city. In 1809, the toast at the society's annual dinner ran: 'To the memory of St Nicholas. May the virtuous habits and simple manners of our Dutch ancestors be not lost in the luxuries and refinements of the present time.'

Irving's *History of New-York* was hugely successful, making his name, but also clouding its comic origins. Instead, the book began to be read as though it described real events. The *History* claimed that the first church in New Amsterdam was dedicated to St Nicholas, in honour of the colonists' patron saint, and, sure enough, half a century later, this was repeated as fact in a history of New York. (In actuality, there was no New York church named for St Nicholas until the twentieth century.) Had anyone paused to check, the *History* could not have passed as history for a moment: Irving described 'Dutch' New York cookies being impressed with, on one side, an image of Rip van Dam, the lieutenant-governor of New Amsterdam, on the other 'the noted St. Nicholas, vulgarly called Sancteclaus . . . venerated by true Hollanders.' The historical Rip van Dam was indeed a New York politician, but one who had governed years after Dutch New Amsterdam had turned into British New York.

Yet the Nicholas legend-building continued. In 1810, for the next St Nicholas dinner, Pintard produced a broadside bearing an engraving of 'the good holy man' St Nicholas in his bishop's robes, holding his bags of gold, and, next to it, pictures of good and bad children by a fireplace hung with stockings.* Underneath was a verse, in Dutch and in English:

> St Nicholas, my dear good friend!
> To serve you ever was my end,

---

* The phrase 'De Goedheiligman' is used today in the Netherlands to refer to the saint; I have been unable to determine if it was in use before Pintard, or whether this was a New World borrowing.

If you will, now, me something give,
I'll serve you ever while I live.

Pintard claimed this verse had been recited to him by 'an ancient lady 87 years of age'. It is possible, of course, that Pintard did hear it from an elderly Dutch lady, although if she had been eighty-seven in 1810, not only had she been born in an English colony, but so had her parents. It seems likely, therefore, that Pintard invented the verses, and possibly even the old lady, for the verses included one detail that had not previously been known in the Netherlands: that the saint lived in Spain the rest of the year. By later in the nineteenth century, this tradition was a regular feature of Dutch descriptions of 'their' St Nicholas, but there is no evidence of it appearing in the Low Countries before Pintard's broadside.

Legend, however, easily trumped fact. Two weeks after that dinner, the *New York Spectator* published a poem about the 'good holy man' – the Dutch phrase repeated by Pintard – adding: 'whom we Sancte Claus name'. The poem, too, concentrated on the Dutch roots of the city, its saint bringing not apples, as he did in German lands, but a 'bright Orange', tipping its hat to the Dutch princes of Orange-Nassau. (It is noticeable too that these English-speaking authors all used versions the German word *Sankt*, not the Dutch *Sint*.) Two years later, knowledge of Sancte Claus had spread widely enough for a censorious volume for children, *False Stories Corrected*, to dismiss 'Old Santa-claw, of whom so often little children hear such foolish stories; and once in the year are encouraged to hang their stockings in the Chimney at night'. By 1830 he was firmly enough established that a New York bookseller advertised that in his 'Temple' of 'Santaclaus' customers could return to 'the good ways of their fathers': less than twenty-one years after his American birth, he was already a piece of nostalgia.

So it appears Washington Irving, John Pintard and their friends should be credited with the creation of Santa Claus. Or should they? Almost everything suggests that they were the creators – were it not for two references in a New York newspaper to 'Santa Claus' in 1773 and 1774, the first appearing when John Pintard was fourteen, and Irving not yet born. Once more we need to stop and rewind.

On 23 December 1773 *Rivington's New-York Gazetteer* reported: 'Last Monday the anniversary of St. Nicholas, otherwise called Santa Claus, was celebrated at Protestant Hall . . . where a great number of sons of that ancient saint celebrated the day with great joy and festivity.' There was a similar mention in 1774, followed by decades of silence.

'Last' Monday might have been the 20th, or possibly the 13th, of December. What it wasn't was 6 December, just as, later, the New-York Historical Society took an elastic approach to the saint's day, their annual dinner by no means always falling on 6 December. The meeting at the Protestant Hall, 'at Mr. Samuel Waldron's, on Long Island', makes it sound as if Mr Waldron might have been running a pub with a meeting-room attached. (He also hosted St Patrick's Day events, so the 'Protestant' part seems nominal.) It is unlikely that this was an anti-British group, as *Rivington's Gazetteer* was published by John Rivington, a loyalist so famously stalwart he was hanged in effigy by the Sons of Liberty in 1775. Where, then, did this St Nicholas group, who used the name 'Santa Claus', come from? No explanation, nor even any guess, has ever been put forward. It might be, however, that it was another immigrant group, neither Dutch, nor pseudo-Dutch, which supplies the missing link between St Nicholas and Santa.

By the eighteenth century the European settlers of what would soon be New York State included immigrants from what are today Germany and Austria, from the Czech lands, from Scandinavia and Finland, as well as from Britain. Switzerland, too, had seen a mass migration to the New World, with possibly as many as 25,000 Swiss heading for North Carolina, Pennsylvania and New York in that century alone. Many came from their country's German-speaking regions, a fact which becomes of potential interest to Santa Claus historians when we remember that two of the Swiss-German, or Schweizerdeutsch, dialect names for St Nicholas were Samichlaus and Santi-Chlaus, both of which sound far closer to Santa Claus than Sint Nicolaas does.

Samichlaus travelled through the Swiss mountains on St Nicholas's Day as early as the seventeenth century. We cannot, of course, be certain, but there were Swiss immigrants in New York, they came from the part of the world that celebrated the visit of Samichlaus, and it is therefore entirely possible that this Swiss dialect name is the ancestor of Santa Claus, transmitted via *Rivington's Gazetteer*, a copy of which we know John Pintard himself owned.

Other parts of the new holiday traditions, after all, came from similarly transplanted customs. From the very earliest days of the Pintard/Irving version, stockings were the receptacles for presents, taken for granted by later use so that there has rarely been any discussion about the origin of this custom. Some have located it in the Dutch practice whereby children treated their shoes or clogs as gift-receptacles, the shape of the shoe a reminder of the saint's travel by ship to the Netherlands. Yet if Pintard was indeed the creator of the Spanish home of St Nicholas, then this must also be a later addition to the canon. Irving, in his *Knickerbocker History* in 1809, simply wrote that the 'pious' stocking-hanging ceremony was 'still religiously observed in all our ancient families'.

It is possible that either Pintard or Irving invented the idea. In Britain, an anthology printed in 1812–13 attributed the custom to either Italy or Spain, which it seemed to consider were potentially the same place: 'Italian nobles had a practice called "ZAPATA", (the Spanish for a *Shoe*)', wherein they placed 'in the slippers or stockings of persons they wished to honour, some present of dress or trinkets'.

A decade later, an almanac recorded that on Epiphany, Venetian children hung stockings in the kitchen for La Befana to fill with 'dirt, rubbish and a few sweetmeats'. The same year *The Children's Friend* illustrated stockings hanging ready for 'Santeclaus', as well as showing Santeclaus' sled,

complete with reindeer, the first time these appeared in connection with Christmas or the bringer of gifts.* *The Children's Friend* may also have influenced Pintard's friend Clement Clarke Moore, whose 'A Visit from St Nicholas'

---

* This is not the 1780 book of that title published in Boston (mentioned on p. 94), but one published in New York in 1821. As well as the 'firsts' mentioned above, it was the first book in the new world to be printed with lithographs, a technological innovation that would ultimately lead to inexpensive colour printing – important for the colour of Santa's suit. It has been suggested that the book's author might have been James Paulding, the brother-in-law of Washington Irving and himself a formidable promoter of the St Nicholas-is-New-Amsterdam-Dutch school.

was written in 1822, because Moore's poem had both stockings and reindeer, which were now given names (although not Rudolph, who had to wait a century to join his reindeer friends). And, like the New-York Historical Society, Moore was not overly committed to marking the actual saint's day, following *The Children's Friend* by relocating it from the eve of 6 December to the eve of the 25th, and the success of this work made the 5 December date almost immediately obsolete.

Now Santa put toys, fruit and nuts in the stockings of good children, while bad children got coal, or birch switches, which was better than back in Zurich, where bad children received horse manure and rotten vines (although not yet in stockings).

In Zurich, Samichlaus also brought trees for all children, while in Germany the Christmas tree remained, for the moment, something for the prosperous and the urban. The less prosperous became familiar with the custom in institutions – in schools, hospitals, orphanages and the like – where they had become a feature of charitable giving: patrons and donors attended candle-lighting ceremonies, at which carols were sung and gifts were handed to the poor.

Traditions in private houses were not dissimilar. In 1798 the English poet Samuel Taylor Coleridge visited a family in Ratzeburg, in north Germany. On Christmas Eve, the children took over the parlour, where 'a great yew bough . . . [was] fastened on the Table' and decorated with 'a multitude of little Tapers . . . and coloured paper, &c.' The children laid out their presents underneath, before inviting their parents in. The following day, the situation was reversed, and the parents laid out the children's gifts by the bough. The trees, the decorations and presents varied from family to family, from place to place.

However the evening was staged, in the nineteenth century the custom appeared more frequently, at first in the very highest echelons of society. Henrietta of Nassau-Weilburg, born in Prussia, erected a tree in Vienna in 1816 after her marriage to Archduke Charles of Austria; twenty years later, Helen of Mecklenburg did the same when she moved to Paris on her marriage to the duc d'Orléans. Soon the less fashionable followed, and trees were also found in the homes of the elite in Denmark and Norway, in Finland and Sweden, and in the Netherlands.

In England, Princess Lieven, born into a Baltic German family in Riga, where one of the very earliest trees was recorded, spent the Christmas of 1829 at Earl Cowper's house near Hertford, and 'got up a little *fête* such as is customary all over Germany', wrote the memoirist Charles Greville.* 'Three large trees in great pots were put upon a

long table covered with pink linen; each tree was illuminated with three circular tiers of coloured wax candles – blue, green, red, and white.' Below each tree were toys,

* Charles Cavendish Fulke Greville (1794–1865) was in life an apparently harmless member of the upper classes, known mainly for being a good cricketer. However, when his diary, which he kept for over forty years, was published on his instructions after his death, it left many, like Queen Victoria, '*horrified* and *indignant* at this dreadful and really scandalous book. Mr Greville's indiscretion, indelicacy, ingratitude, betrayal of confidence and shameful disloyalty towards his Sovereign make it *very important* that the book should be severely censored and discredited', particularly as 'The tone in which he speaks of royalty is . . . most reprehensible.' For once Queen Victoria was correct: it is his complete lack of deference that makes the book such a delight.

gloves, handkerchiefs, workboxes and books for the individuals tree's 'owner'. Queen Adelaide, the wife of William IV, from Saxe-Meiningen in south-western Germany, had a tree on Christmas Eve at Brighton Pavilion, and the young Princess Victoria and her mother, the Duchess of Kent, also German-born, had 'large round tables on which were placed the trees hung with lights and sugar ornaments' at Kensington Palace.

Coleridge's published an essay on his German Christmas experience in 1809 in his own journal, *The Friend*, which had a limited audience. By 1810, however, it had been reprinted in three London papers; in 1825, in a popular annual; in 1828, in the *Gentleman's Magazine*; and in 1834 it was reprinted in *The Times*. A number of extracts also appeared in local British newspapers, as well as in several American ones. By 1844 the English translation of a German children's Christmas book, with its frontispiece of a decorated fir tree, and its notes on 'The German form of celebrating Christmas Eve', appeared with Coleridge's essay at the end. Thanks to its popularity, a single family's local tradition was known across the English-speaking world as though it were the standard way Christmas was celebrated throughout Germany.

All of this was overtaken in 1848, when the *Illustrated London News* published an engraving of Victoria and Albert beside a tabletop tree at Windsor. The accompanying text explained that this was the children's tree, while the queen, the prince consort, the Duchess of Kent, and 'the royal household' all had their own, as well as additional trees in the dining-room.* This single image cemented the

---

* The illustration shows the gifts, but there was no mention of

Christmas tree in the popular consciousness, so much so that by 1861, the year of Albert's death, it was firmly believed that this German prince had transplanted the custom to England with him when he married. In the USA, the engraving was rendered more democratic when *Godey's Lady's Book*, the bestselling monthly magazine in the country, reprinted it in 1850, merely removing Victoria's jewellery and Albert's sash and medals (as well as his moustache), and reducing the number of presents under the tree. The illustration was retitled 'The Christmas Tree', with no reference to royalty, the 'the' suggesting only one tree per household, not the small forest set up every year at Windsor.

The image was reprinted in 1860, and again in the following decade. By then, Christmas trees had taken root in American culture in a way they would not do in Britain for a century (one estimate in 1930 thought 4 million trees were erected that year, in a population of approximately 45 million). For a start, they were not a fashion set by the aristocracy, but one generated by the people. In legend, just as Prince Albert took the Christmas tree to England, so in the USA it was said that Hessian soldiers fighting with the British in the Revolutionary Wars had been decorating their traditional Christmas trees when Washington crossed the Delaware on 26 December 1776, making it possible for him to take them by surprise and win the crucial Battle of Trenton. Given our knowledge of Christmas in Germany, which centred around 24 December, not the 26th, this is

---

when they were given. Other sources tell us that the queen continued to give presents at New Year, not on Christmas Eve or Christmas Day, until her death in 1901.

unlikely. But Christmas trees may have arrived in North America as early as 1786. In North Carolina that year, a member of the Moravian Brethren accused an apprentice of cutting down a small pine tree on Christmas Eve, the day on which trees were customarily erected in Germany. It was one, he added, 'which he had been taking special care of'. In 1805, this time in Georgia, the students at a Moravian Indian Mission school were taken on an outing 'to fetch a small green tree for Christmas'. The following year, they again 'fetch[ed] shrubs and little trees for the Christmas decorations', some of which might have been used in constructing Putzes. And in 1812, they went to a friend's house where there was 'a treat for our young ones . . . a little decorated tree'.

'Little decorated trees' were found in the North, too. One is shown in a watercolour by Lewis Miller, a Pennsylvania folk artist, which included the date 1809. Since Miller would have been only thirteen in that year, it is likely the date indicates a later recollection of a Philadelphia family Christmas at that time. The tree itself, decorated with fruit and paper cutouts or possibly verses, is unmistakably labelled 'Christmas tree'. (The naked child under the table is, more mysteriously, 'A Christmas Gift': a nativity reference, or just a child born in December?)

In 1821 in Lancaster, Pennsylvania, one resident recorded in his diary that his children were going to the sawmill 'for Christmas trees' – he felt no need to expand, as though by then everyone knew what a Christmas tree was, and that was likely to be the case, at least locally, since in 1823, the bachelors of York, Pennsylvania announced plans for a charity '*Krischkintle Bauhm*', which they promised would be 'superb, superfine, superfrostical, schnockagastical, double

Lewis Miller, 'An 1809 Christmas in York, Pennsylvania' (*Collection of the York County Heritage Trust, York, Pennsylvania*). In a mixture of German and English, Miller wrote: 'Seifert, the Blue dier, colouring, dying, and Family, in north George Street, 1809. She mentioned – This morning I haven't yet swept the floor.' Then, presumably listing out the holiday meal, 'Beef, broth, salad, eggs and good wine is good for the children.'

refined, mill-twill'd made of Dog's Wool, Swingling Tow, and Posnum [Possum?] fur'.*

From now on, Christmas trees were recorded with increasing frequency: first in areas of German emigration; by 1843, the *New York Tribune* was carrying advertisements for trees; and in 1851, the city's Washington market set

---

* This marks the beginning of the evolution of the Christ child, *Christkind* in German, *Christkindl* as a diminutive, into Kris Kringle. In 1830, one Pennsylvania resident referred to Christ-kinkle nights, and by 1837, children waited for Christkingle. In 1842, two books

aside space for their sale. Trees had reached the Midwest by the 1840s: Calvin Fletcher, an Indianapolis lawyer, land speculator and banker, described his family's 'Christmass Gifts . . . hung on a tree in the parlor'. (Despite the casual familiarity with which he describes the setting, this is the first year he writes of having a tree.) Trees were erected by German immigrants in Texas in the 1840s, and by the 1850s they had become naturalized and were decorated with local produce: moss, cotton, pecans, red pepper swags and, an American innovation, the popcorn string, as well as Old World red berries, biscuits and sweets.

Americans also began to innovate by recreating the idea of a public tree, a tree erected and decorated for the benefit of all. Initially these trees were put up by groups affiliated to churches, with tickets sold for the benefit of the church or other charitable organization, as with the York bachelors. As early as 1830, a Dorcas Society, also in York, had what the local newspaper described as a 'famous' tree as the centrepiece for their Christmas bazaar.* Fairs to raise funds for the abolitionist movement also advertised

---

were published in Philadelphia, *Kriss Kringle's Book* and *Kriss Kringle's Christmas Tree: A holliday* [sic] *present for boys and girls*. By this time, all of the German elements of the Christkind had vanished, and Kris Kringle had become another name for Santa Claus, a bearded old man with a sleigh pulled by reindeer. By 1848, a Midwestern bank director used Kris Kringle as a synonym for Santa without explanation.

* Some assume this indicated the renown of German trees; I suspect, however, that the word 'famous' was being used colloquially, as an expression of approval. Dorcas Societies took their name from the woman in Acts 9:36–9 who was 'full of good works and almsdeeds': usually formed around church groups, Dorcas societies made clothes for the poor.

trees. Gradually, from the fund-raising side of religion, they moved to the educational, as Sunday schools began to erect trees from the late 1840s. Soon trees came to be considered essential parts of a religious Christmas display, but they were open to private enterprise too. The Goodridge Brothers, barbers and shopkeepers in York, as grandsons of a slave woman and a white man, may have been involved in abolitionist causes, but tickets to view their 1840 tree were advertised without any reference other than the commercial.

Christmas trees were swiftly becoming symbols of something intangible and indefinable: partly of middle-class domesticity, but partly expressions of nationhood. The tree took on national status after New Hampshire-born President Franklin Pierce chose to have one in the White House in 1856. In the next decade many more were exposed to trees during the Civil War, when soldiers were garrisoned with people from other parts of the country. Even in wartime, the trees remained domestic symbols, especially as expressed by *Harper's Weekly*, the country's most widely circulated magazine at the time.

Many purchased the magazine for its extensive coverage of the war, in which the illustrations of Thomas Nast were prominent. Nast (1840–1902) was the creator of the American political cartoon and the first to use an elephant to represent the US Republican party. Political cartoonists generally have a shelf-life: once the events of the day are forgotten, so are they. Nast, however, has lived on, as the originator of the twentieth – and so far, the twenty-first – century's image of Santa Claus.

Santa had taken a little while to get there. In his *Knicker-bocker History*, Washington Irving describes how St Nicholas behaved – rattling by horse and wagon over rooftops and going down chimneys to place presents in stockings, laying his finger to the side of his nose in a gesture beseeching silence before he left – but he doesn't describe his appearance. Others had their own views. In 1815 the *New York Evening Post* ran a 'proclamation' from Santa Claus, signed, 'Santa Claus, Queen and Empress of all handsome girls . . . Queen and Empress of the Court of Fashions', followed by approval from this 'good, delightful, charming' woman's husband, St Nicholas. (This gender-swap never became popular.) Another version appeared in a North Carolina newspaper of the 1850s, which said he was a 'coster' [costermonger, or street-seller of fruit and vegetables] who breathed fire on bad children through a keyhole.

The Children's Friend in 1821 contained the first illustration of 'Old Santeclaus': a tiny bearded young man, driving a tiny reindeer-drawn sleigh beside a towering chimney. Clement Clarke Moore filled in some gaps. His 'St Nick' is an elf with a 'little round belly', who wears fur, smokes a pipe and carries a pedlar's pack filled with toys. (In a direct borrowing from Irving, he also puts 'his finger aside of his nose'.) In the first illustrations of the poem, in 1848, Moore's saint wears old-fashioned Dutch clothes, but although still small and round, he is no longer an elf. His appearance then became established: in *The Lamplighter*, Maria Susanna Cummins's bestseller (only *Uncle Tom's Cabin* sold more copies in its first year of publication), 'the veteran toy-dealer' continued to wear his fur cap and smoke his Dutch pipe.*

* The success of *The Lamplighter*, first published in 1854, must also have promoted the American Santa across Europe, as the book was translated into French, German, Italian and Danish. This was not

Thomas Nast changed all that. Nast was born, like so many other figures that populate Christmas, in Germany, in Landau. Many have suggested that he drew on childhood memories of Pelz Nichol for his iconic illustrations. However, Nast left Germany at the age of six, so his memories would have been hazy at best; furthermore, the Christmas gift-bringer in Landau in the early 1840s was not Pelz Nichol; and, finally, Nast grew up in New York exactly at the period when the St Nicholas of Irving, Paulding and Moore was becoming established – surely a likelier source of inspiration.

It was also in New York that Christmas was becoming increasingly child-centred, as seen in the softening of the stern bishop into a 'jolly old elf'. Perhaps the rowdy street portions of the holiday, the older topsy-turvy traditions when apprentices shook free of their masters, were being replicated after a fashion as children replaced their parents as the day's star performers. Now the man with the sack, a toy-pedlar, and therefore of the working class, was, like the apprentices of former times, going house to house, but instead of demanding money, he was freely giving things without payment. Possibly Santa-as-benefactor appealed to Nast, for as a cartoonist, he revelled in unmasking political corruption and the oppression of the poor.

Nast's first Christmas spread for *Harper's*, in 1862, was not of Santa, nor of St Nicholas, but of soldiers separated from their families, a domestic reading of Christmas that

---

Santa's first journey across the Atlantic, however. He had travelled to England soon after Moore's poem was published in 1823: in 1827, the *Gentleman's Magazine* referred to 'the ideal Sandy Claus of the American children', giving his Dutch ancestry while adding that 'in the opinion of the majority', he was 'a little old negro'.

was only to grow in importance in the Civil War. The following year his first Santa Claus was sheer Union propaganda. 'Santa Claus in Camp' wears a stars-and-stripes outfit, but he is not the focus of the engraving: the Union soldiers filling the page are. And while a banner reads 'Welcome Santa Claus', it is secondary to a much larger American flag. Yet here, too, the domestic theme resonates. Santa hands out gifts for the soldiers – socks, toys – that act as reminders of home and children. In case the point was not clear, the next engraving was entitled 'Christmas Eve 1862', and showed a woman at home praying over her sleeping children, herself overlooked by a picture of a man on the wall wreathed in holly, presumably the soldier in the next picture, who in turn stares at a portrait of a woman and children. And, in little vignettes binding together the divided family, Santa climbs down a chimney, and then flies over the camp, tossing out presents. The following year, the same theme of families divided and united continues, as 'Furlough' shows a couple kissing under mistletoe as their children dance about them in front of a tree. Around them, roundels stress the central aspects of the season: a snowy winter scene, Santa coming down the chimney, children emptying their stockings, a Christmas dinner – and, oh yes, a tiny nativity scene.

In these early depictions, Nast's Santa does not bear much resemblance to our image today. He is very short, often little bigger than a child. He is dark, and wears dark fur hats that cover much of his forehead, leaving little of his face visible. Later he has a Dutch-style long-stemmed pipe. In 1866 he is still elf-sized, standing on a chair to reach a tabletop, while his ledger with the names of good and bad children is larger than he is. But now he has a

workshop, and lives in a northerly ice palace, and his beard
has grown bushier, and whiter.* *The Children's Friend* shows
him in a sort of Cossack fur hat; other illustrators gave
him a tall peaked hat, or a cloth cap with a tassel. His
round cheeks and white-fur-trimmed suit took longer to
establish, becoming a signature of Nast's Santa only in the

1880s. Nast continued to be influenced by current events.
His journalistic crusade against the corrupt New York
politician 'Boss' Tweed might perhaps have influenced his
depiction of Santa, with his overhanging balcony of a
belly, while the cartoonist himself allowed that his Santa's
rosy face came from Bacchus, the mythological god of
wine, and his rich furs from the plutocratic slum-landlord
and Tweed-supporter, John Jacob Astor.

Nor was the colour of Santa's clothes yet settled. In
1837 the painter Robert Weir, a friend of Irving, had
painted Santa in a red cloak worn over a dark Dutch suit,
and brown boots.† In 1856 the *British Mother's Journal*
dressed him in 'his yellow Christmas coat', the 'his' suggesting that the writer thought yellow was the traditional

---

* The origins of Santa's home at the North Pole are uncertain: it
was possibly by association with his reindeer. Another historian has
suggested that Santa moved to the North Pole after the fate of the
expedition to discover the Northwest Passage, led by John Franklin,
was revealed in the 1850s. If so, a substantial gap in time inter-
vened.

† The picture was painted while Weir was a drawing master at
West Point military academy. It can't be said if his most prominent
artist pupil, James McNeill Whistler, saw it or not, but over the
course of his career his other students formed a cavalcade of
American history: Jefferson Davis, Stonewall Jackson, Robert E.
Lee, George Armstrong Custer, William Tecumseh Sherman and
Ulysses S. Grant.

colour. Nast's engravings of the 1860s and 1870s were in black and white, and so all that is possible to say is that Santa's clothes were dark.

By now, Santa had become substantially different from all other Christmas gift-bringers. He had no religious associations, unlike St Nicholas or the Christkind; he had no punitive role – he might threaten to withhold presents from bad children, but he never actually did so, nor did he carry implements of punishment; he was no longer an outsider, as the various earlier sidekicks and wild men had been; and he brought substantial gifts, not just fruit and nuts. He is perhaps a reversed-out image of Christ, almost a photographic negative: Santa is fat (Christ is almost always depicted as a thin man); he is old (on 25 December Christ is, of course, a newborn); he wears red (white); lives at the North Pole (Middle East); is married (single); owns a factory (is a carpenter) that produces luxury goods (turning water into wine is arguably as close as Christ got). In short, Santa had become the god of hedonistic enjoyment, the exact opposite of the man who preached that it is 'easier for a camel to go through the eye of a needle, than for a rich man to enter into the kingdom of God'.

And to bring his largesse, Santa had, from nearly the beginning, a great sack for his presents, whether from St Nicholas's sacks of gold, or the pedlar of *The Children's Friend*. As early as 1826, on New Year's Day, New Yorkers' formal holiday visits were disrupted. Normally, genteel society paid calls on their friends, pausing for a drink and taking a single 'cookey' for the road. But on this day, two men were spotted with 'a large bag, on one side of which was a full-length portrait of Santa Claus', into which they were stowing great handfuls of cookies. Order was restored, however, when it was realized that their ultimate destination was a local orphanage. Because by the 1820s, 'Carousals', as *The Times* referred to the drunken revelry of the past, were no longer enjoyed in the streets, and the holiday was spent as a family 'round a warm and comfortable hearth'.

The king of the family hearth, and of charity, of the new Christmas of children, was, of course, Charles Dickens. In *A Christmas Carol* (1843), which has often been described as the book that 'invented' Christmas, the domestic hearth, and the fires that cook the Christmas dinner, represent all that is good in the season.*

---

* A swift plot summary of the book, for those who have managed to avoid any of its hundreds, if not thousands, of adaptations. *A Christmas Carol* opens seven years after the death of Jacob Marley, Scrooge's business partner. Scrooge despises Christmas with its, to him, false expressions of goodwill. He refuses to join his family's Christmas party, and rejects solicitations for Christmas charity. The most he will do is grudgingly give his clerk, Bob Cratchit, a single day off. On Christmas Eve, he is visited by the ghost of Marley, doomed to walk the earth dragging the chains he forged during a life spent dedicated to accumulating wealth. Instead of business, he tells Scrooge, it was 'Mankind [that was] was my business. The common welfare was my business; charity, mercy, forbearance, and benevolence, were, all, my business.' To avoid the same fate, Scrooge must heed the ghosts of Christmas Past, Present and Yet to Come. The Ghost of Christmas Past takes Scrooge to revisit his lonely childhood, and the day his fiancée leaves him, claiming that he loves money more than her. The Ghost of Christmas Present then shows the material lack and emotional riches of the Christmases of working men and women, including the Cratchits' Christmas dinner, enjoyed despite their poverty and the serious illness of their small son, Tiny Tim. The Ghost of Christmas Yet to

Dickens, and *A Christmas Carol*, were heavily influenced, as so many were, by Washington Irving. Not, in this case, his *Knickerbocker History*, but by a book that has been more or less forgotten, the unenticingly titled *The Sketch Book of Geoffrey Crayon, Gent.* Irving's family business had suffered during the War of 1812, and in 1815 he set off for Europe in an attempt to establish trading connections. As his *Knickerbocker History* is an imagined history of an idealized past New York, so *The Sketch Book* (1819) is an imagined past England, told in the persona of a middle-aged American visitor.

At Christmas the narrator visits Bracebridge Hall in Yorkshire, where he is welcomed by an Olde Worlde squire who cleaves to Christmas customs 'daily growing more and more faint': the squire feasts his tenants, who play games and dance, there is mumming, a Lord of Misrule, holly, ivy and mistletoe, mince pies and roast beef, a boar's head and home-brewed beer and parlour games, and everyone is endlessly happy.

The book was as successful as the *Knickerbocker History* had been, going through at least seventeen editions on both sides of the Atlantic over the next half-century. Apart from the sheer *joie-de-vivre* of the writing, Irving tapped into the new passion for antiquarianism. But because the book

---

Come shows Scrooge his own lonely, unmourned death; in contrast, Tiny Tim's death devastates his family. Scrooge begs for the chance to reform, and in the morning, sets all in motion: he sends a turkey to the Cratchits, he reconciles with his family and increases Bob Cratchit's wages. He becomes a 'second father' to Tiny Tim, 'who did NOT die', and ever after, 'it was always said of him, that he knew how to keep Christmas well, if any man alive possessed the knowledge. May that be truly said of us, and all of us! And so, as Tiny Tim observed, God bless Us, Every One!'

was written as a travelogue, the knowledge that it was fiction vanished as quickly as had the satire of his history of New York. British readers understood that it did not describe their own Christmases, but typically thought that it was an accurate description of Christmases past, while American reviewers took the book as straightforward reportage.[*]

Yet by looking backwards, Irving somehow managed to help create the Christmas of the future, the Christmas of modernity.

---

[*] One of the strangest consequences of this misunderstanding is the long-running Bracebridge Dinner, held annually at Yosemite National Park, in California. In 1927, slow bookings prompted a local hotel to stage an evening's entertainment based on Irving's stories, hosted by 'Squire Bracebridge' himself, with a newly invented 'Lord Neville Bracebridge'. Equally invented were many other details of the evening, which at one and the same time is described as being set in 1718 and in the Renaissance, although one twentieth-century director of the show described it as 'vaguely Elizabethan'. Irving, however, was not its only brush with greatness. The photographer Ansel Adams directed the event for nearly half a century, once playing the role of the jester (it is perhaps needless to say that there is no such character in Irving). Today, seven or eight dinners are held each December, bookable as part of a package with a stay at the hotel.

Chapter Seven

To our twenty-first-century eyes, Washington Irving and Charles Dickens are not modern; they represent the Good Old Days. But it is in Dickens, especially, that Christmas first meets the modern world. Indeed, it is Dickens who showed the world that modernity and Christmas are eminently suited to each other.

In his first novel, *The Pickwick Papers* (1836/7), Dickens sends his characters to spend an idyllic old-fashioned Christmas in the country: the focus is on Christmas Eve, not the day itself; they drink punch and tell ghost stories; the single 'carol' is a song about spring – in short, the holiday is about country hospitality, food and drink and merriment, all for adults. In the same year, the essayist Leigh Hunt wrote on 'The Inexhaustibility of Christmas', listing the accompaniments to the holiday of which he thought no sensible person should ever tire: he gave food twelve entries; games thirteen; pastimes such as carols and waits six; home-based pastimes six; greenery three; drink three; mischief a possible two; money or gifts the same; theatre and cards one each.* What is notable when

---

* He also devotes just seven of the essay's 482 lines to religion; John Bull gets five.

'Old Christmas Festivities', from William Sandys'
Christmastide, its History, Festivities, and Carols (1852).

compared to the past is how little space he gives to drinking, and to street or outdoor rowdy events.

A book on Christmas through the centuries, published in 1852, presents this change in graphic form. Two illustrations, ten pages apart, show 'Old Christmas Festivities' and a modern 'Christmas Tree'.

The former is set in what looks like a pub or a tavern – there is a keg of beer on the floor, alongside discarded tankards, and the crowd, predominantly male, raise their drinks to toast a kissing couple under an enormous bunch of mistletoe or a kissing bough. There are few children visible, one of whom, the potboy, is working. In the second image, we are transported to a middle-class urban drawing room: the focal point, the ceiling-high tree, stands on an expensive-looking carpet, while the stylishly wallpapered

'The Christmas Tree', William Sandys'
Christmastide, its History, Festivities, and Carols (1852).

walls are hung with paintings. Most of the people in the
room are women or children, with only a scattering of
men, and there is no drink visible. Instead there are presents, toys and what appear to be sweets are being offered
around.

Irving's Bracebridge Hall and Dickens's *Pickwick Papers*
were male events. The squire organized the Bracebridge
festivities; the *Pickwick* Christmas barely nodded to women:
female servants provide food and drink and maintain fires;
middle-class women mostly look decorative. *A Christmas
Carol*, by contrast, presages a Christmas Yet to Come. The
Ghost of Christmas Past shows Scrooge the Christmas
party overseen by his old employer, Fezziwig; the Ghost
of Christmas Present takes him to the dinner hosted by
his nephew Fred. But at the emotional core of the book,

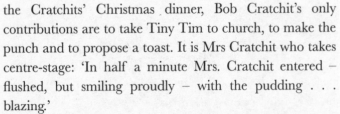

the Cratchits' Christmas dinner, Bob Cratchit's only contributions are to take Tiny Tim to church, to make the punch and to propose a toast. It is Mrs Cratchit who takes centre-stage: 'In half a minute Mrs. Cratchit entered – flushed, but smiling proudly – with the pudding . . . blazing.'

In the original edition, this was not illustrated; by 1876, however, one US edition devoted half its illustrations to the Cratchits, while some adaptations cut the novella down to this single episode. In theatre, too, it became central, with one production ending with a tableau:

> Music: curtains at back are drawn, disclosing 'A Christmas Picture'. In the centre, the GHOST OF XMAS PRESENT, seated as before with his torch raised, red fire blazing . . . R. of CHRISTMAS PRESENT, MRS CRATCHIT, with a pudding in her hands; MARTHA [Cratchit] at her R., with TINY TIM in her arms. Two of the children opposite to them, looking at the pudding. TINY TIM . . . 'God bless us every one!'

Note that Bob Cratchit is nowhere to be seen, much as the March sisters' father, in Louisa May Alcott's *Little Women* (1868/9), was also absent in the book's opening Christmas scene. 'Christmas won't be Christmas without any presents' is the famous first line, but while the absence of presents occupies several pages, the absence of the girls' father is dealt with in a solitary sentence. And when Mr March returns, at a later Christmas, he is introduced as 'another Christmas present for the March family' – he has become something to be handed over, rather than the organizer of the holiday, its Squire Bracebridge.

The Marches celebrate at home, as a nuclear family, only briefly calling on neighbours and making charitable excursions. In this they echo the characters in *A Christmas Carol*: the Cratchits too have no relatives visiting; Scrooge's nephew Fred has lost his mother, but if his father is living, he goes unmentioned, as do his wife's parents. And while the ball given by Fezziwig, the young Scrooge's employer, in theory depicts the old paternal style of Christmas entertainment, in reality it is held at his place of work – in other words, it is an office party.

This is the new world, of offices, of travel, of working late and trying to get home in time for Christmas dinner (Martha Cratchit makes it just in time). Three years after Dickens's book was published, a letter to *The Times* suggested that railway companies should offer special holiday fares, to allow 'a large class of individuals confined . . . in offices, counting-houses, warehouses, shops, &c.' to travel home for Christmas. Yet at the same time, trains were generally metaphors for the alienation and urbanization of the new industrial world – an anti-holiday symbol. The illustrator George Cruikshank depicted this contaminating force graphically: 'Oh my beef, and oh my babies!' despairs the lady of the house as a train bears down on her table, with both her children and her Christmas pudding under threat from modernity.

In the face of this, *A Christmas Carol* permitted a new way of thinking about Christmas. No longer did it have to be the Christmas of Olde England, where the Irvingesque squire was in his manor house and all was right with the world. Now it could be a Christmas where working people travelled home by public transport from counting-houses and offices, where charity was the remit of the rising middle classes, not of the gentry taking care of their own tenants. Dickens took the changes to industrial society – office and factory work, urban poverty and want, food that was bought in shops, not grown in kitchen-gardens, cooked in laundry-coppers and commercial cookshops, not by servants in great halls – he took this new consumerist society, and through Scrooge's 'conversion', he turned it into a sacred duty. Following his lead – cooking the turkey, playing games, drinking toasts, or buying a toy for your child – became the quasi-religious observances of the new middle-class domesticity.

Dickens was an idealist, but he was not naive. He knew that what we want Christmas to be is not what it really is. In *Great Expectations*, written two decades after *A Christmas Carol*, he depicts a *real* Christmas. The novel opens on Christmas Eve, with the orphan Pip terrorized into stealing food and a file to cut through the chains of an escaped convict. The Christmas greeting he receives from his abusive sister is, 'Where the deuce ha' you been?' Every mouthful of his holiday dinner is grudged him, even as the adults speak empty words of charity. It is in retrospect, as an adult, that he, and the reader, can understand the real Christmas that is taking place: the food he steals for the convict, Magwitch, is his real Christmas dinner, the file his gift, and family love is expressed when Magwitch calls him 'my boy'; charity is practised not preached when, to protect Pip from his sister, Magwitch swears he stole the food himself.

Irving, and Dickens even more so, have both been hailed as the inventors of the holiday. That this cannot be true is obvious on rereading their books, which rely on their readers' knowledge of the many customs they do not feel the need to explain.* Instead, it is Squire Bracebridge's love and Scrooge's disdain for the day that reveal the importance Christmas had long assumed: the squire's view is presented as obviously correct, while Scrooge is just as obviously ripe for conversion. One of the most telling clues to the already pervasive recognition of Christmas as a time for giving is that both books were what we today call gift books, books designed specifically to be given as presents, where the focus is on appearance as much as content. The first edition of *A Christmas Carol* had holly and ivy embossed in gold on its covers, while the Christmas chapters from Irving's *Sketch Book* were reprinted in stand-alone editions with titles like *An Old-Fashioned Christmas* and *Old Christmas*, with added illustrations.[†]

Both Irving and Dickens were writing for a market that had been growing for some time. In the eighteenth century, booksellers began to publish special ranges for purchase as New Year's gifts. Almanacs, containing weather forecasts, church holidays, tidal information and dates for planting and harvests, often interspersed with witty sayings, poems

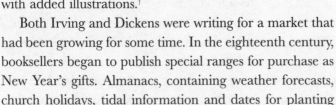

---

* A tiny, but perhaps telling, example of the importance of Christmas in popular culture before Dickens can be found in a police-court report of 1834, where a servant named Edward Christmas Day was accused of robbery. Presumably his parents, Mr and Mrs Day, had found the holiday prominent enough that they gave their son his unusual middle name, to render his surname festive.

[†] In part, it was *A Christmas Carol*'s production standards that gave rise to the idea the book had been a failure on publication. It actually sold extremely well – 6,000 copies in one week, and five printings in the first five months. But the expensive binding, and resulting high production costs, meant that the ratio of income to sales was skewed: sales were good, but the author made less money than he expected.

or proverbs, had been popular from the sixteenth century: *Poor Robin's Almanack* in England from the seventeenth century, and *Poor Richard's* in the colonies in the eighteenth, were two famous examples. These were now joined by books for children, in the eighteenth century always either moralistic, concerning religious education, or educational, all 'very proper for Christmas and New-Year's Gifts', the newspaper advertisements promised. In England by the end of the century, books might be presented as a 'Pleasant Pastime for a Christmas Eve' (although a later offering entitled *Errors and their Consequences* sounds less enticing). By 1829, one children's book tells the story of a curate who gives a book to the children of the poor parish clerk as 'their Christmas gift', his phrasing implying that gifts to children were routine, as routine as the gift being a book. German Christmas books took a similar path, books on proper behaviour gradually giving way to stories, history, the adventures of great men and so on. At the same period, a more elite, more feminine and much more expensive product was placed on the Christmas shelf, in Britain from 1822 and in America from 1826: the annual. These were expensive anthologies of lightweight short stories, poetry and pretty engravings, intended primarily for women and often edited by women too. By 1828, fifteen different annuals sold over 100,000 copies between them.*

---

* For those who say that today's Christmas begins earlier every year, the anodyne necklace advertisement of 1728 (p. 96) was printed in late November, while as early as the 1820s advertisements for annuals were not unknown in October. By the end of the century, *Die Reklame* [The Advertisement], a German trade magazine, warned that after early December, shoppers were too worn out to

While these annuals were *for* Christmas, they were not *about* Christmas. It was children's books in the USA that began the trend: *A Visit from St Nicholas* was both, as was *The Children's Friend* two years earlier. In the early 1840s the idea was now applied to adults, although not at first in fiction. Magazines began to publish special Christmas numbers, a practice begun by the comic magazine *Punch* in 1841. Dickens's *A Christmas Carol* took their idea and applied it to adult literature: now not only children were the recipients of presents at Christmas, about Christmas.

The rise of print culture – of newspapers, magazines, inexpensive broadsides and chapbooks, of song sheets and printed advertising posters – combined with the growth of the new industrial world, where more people worked for cash payments and could afford to purchase these cheaper, mass-produced items. At the same time the rapidly expanding middle classes were having fewer children, and therefore, as we have seen, could concentrate more individual attention on each, leading to the development of the concept of a sheltered childhood spent protected from the brutal outside world, just as women were protected by staying in the home sphere. The increasing importance given to this private sphere and the family it contained was, in cyclical fashion, then promoted in the new books and magazines, which advertised the very items that the model home and family should own.

Christmas, as we have seen, had always been a time of

---

act on new advertisements. In 1929 a consortium of retailers in Los Angeles promoted 'the 1929 Wonder of Christmas' in October. In fact, as early as 1661, one almanac took it for granted that preparations began in November, when 'the Cook and the Comfit-maker make ready for Christmass'.

spending. With no lessening in the importance of the Christmas dinner, and an additional focus on gift-giving, that now only increased. Clerks could obtain extra seasonal work 'making out Christmas bills' for shopkeepers, while a court in 1824 heard that one fraudster had spent his illicit gains on paying his mistress's 'Christmas bills for millinery, jewellery, &c.'; in another case the court was petitioned to reschedule a trial, as 'this was the season of the year at which the expenses of the house were necessarily very large'. The *New Monthly Magazine* agreed, groaning that the month of January was made up entirely of fog, wind, sleet and Christmas bills.

In 1802, Queen Charlotte gave a children's Christmas party at Windsor, with the room 'fitted up as a fair', and the toys to be given away set out in booths and stalls. The fairground setting might, perhaps, have been a memory of German Christmas fairs in the queen's former home of Mecklenburg-Strelitz. Otherwise, despite the charitable intent of the evening, the fair conveyed a subliminally commercial message. Rather than Santa contributing

to the commercialization of a previously pure idea of the holiday, did he instead, by bringing toys to children without charge in their homes, rather than delivering them to commercial locations like fairs, remove the sense of a business transaction from Christmas?

Whatever the case, by the end of the nineteenth century Santa was, according to one American magazine, 'our biggest captain of industry'. As early as the 1820s, St Nicholas was being used to sell jewellery in one New York newspaper advertisement, and by the 1840s, Santa had become a regular visitor to various shops: in 1841, 'Criscringle, or Santa Claus' could be caught 'in the very act of descending a chimney' at Parkinson's confectionery shop in Philadelphia; a few years later, the same shop became 'Kriss Kringle's Headquarters'. (It is unclear whether these were men in costume, or printed images.)

Initially, as we have seen, Santa was imagined in a variety of guises: he was a saint, an empress of the court of fashion, a coster. Once the image of Santa portrayed by Thomas Nast spread, however, shops began to share a fairly homogeneous image: a fat bearded older man carrying a sack, travelling in a sleigh pulled by reindeer. It was commercially expedient for a single image to predominate, fostering an immediate link in the customers' minds between the man and the gifts that he might bring if only the customer would enter their shops.

And what were the gifts being purchased? The older view of gifts as hierarchical offerings continued, but now as presents given by parents to children, or by husbands to wives. Far less common were gifts from dependants to the breadwinner, although advertisements for hair oil and dancing pumps offer exceptions to the rule. But in 1809 in one Boston newspaper, of five seasonal advertisements, four were for children's books and toys and one was for women's jewellery: dependants all. Meanwhile the idea of dependants giving gifts to those who provided for them throughout the year remained unusual: one visitor who saw German children giving their parents gifts thought it was 'very peculiar'.

Many industries understood the benefits of season-specific presents: printers of sheet music now produced collections of carols; items of clothing were promoted as suitable for Christmas parties. Other goods, with no discernible Christmas content, were promoted anyway. It is difficult to imagine the joy engendered by receiving a jar of Hubert's Roseate Powder, which 'removes superfluous hairs' in time for 'Christmas festivals'. Soothing syrup for teething babies was sold as 'A real Christmas box'. And there were advertisements where the only holiday element was the headline:

[Advertisement.]—Christmas, or New Year's Gifts.—Robert Wiss (late Hawkins and Co.) respectfully calls the attention of the public to his Patent Portable Self-acting Water-closets, which many years' experience have proved to answer the purpose in every respect,

Books continued to be the most common present for children. *Alice Through the Looking Glass*, wrote Lewis Carroll's publisher, 'must come out for Christmas'. Even when they were published at other times of year, Christmas sales mattered: 'How has the [*Hunting of the*] *Snark* sold during the Xmas Season?' Carroll inquired. '*That* . . . would be a much better test of its success . . . than any amount of sale at its first coming out.'

Other goods with year-round sales were now presented at Christmas in a special, often spectacular, fashion. By the middle of the nineteenth century, the main Berlin Christmas market had become a sad relic of a glorious past, the haunt of sellers of cheap novelties and trinkets, supplemented by even cheaper goods hawked by street-sellers, a Tingel-Tangel (cabaret) and some not-very-covert places to gamble. By the 1870s the size of the market was further reduced, and the resort of the poorer classes, as the more prosperous moved on to patronize permanent shops, especially the new department stores, all of which invested in elaborate seasonal displays. The *Konditorei*, or sweet shops, placed sugar models of battles or replicas of the nearby streets and buildings in their windows. The newspapers promoted the most glamorous displays: from 1826 until 1859, Ludwig Rellstab, a journalist and critic, took an annual *Weihnachtswanderung*, or Christmas stroll, through the streets of Berlin, sharing his thoughts on the shoppers, the merchandise, the ambiance, with the readers of the *Vossische Zeitung*. By the end of the century, what had begun as a personal essay had in other hands become advertising masquerading as editorial content: journalists described shops' toys, furniture, jewellery and other potential presents, complete with lists of prices. The trade magazine *Die Reklame* laid out a plan of campaign to begin each November with a 'collective exhibition' of merchandise that could be covered by their local newspapers under headlines like 'Christmas Sights', or 'Christmas Strolls', giving the illusion of independent journalism.

American shopkeepers started a little later, but then raced ahead. In the 1830s Broadway was New York's premier shopping street, and shop windows were crammed with Christmas merchandise. Soon 'window-dressing' meant more than just piling up goods or, as had been done in Britain, adding greenery and extra lighting. Seasonal set-pieces did not necessarily include goods for sale, they just had to attract attention. In Boston, one shop window contained a Santa Claus complete with sleigh and stuffed reindeer, while a New York toyshop had steam trains running through theirs. R. H. Macy & Co., a rapidly expanding dry-goods store, was on nearby Sixth Avenue, and in 1874 it claimed to have $10,000-worth of dolls in its Christmas display. Macy's innovation was not sheer expenditure, but creating a coherent tableau. One year it was a dolls' croquet party; in 1876, the centennial of American independence, a colonial dolls' outing; in 1889, *Uncle Tom's*

Cabin was the basis for a dramatic winter scene, as Eliza was chased across the ice by bloodhounds.

The development of department stores in many major cities – New York, London, Berlin – produced a new Christmas tradition, that of going to see the Christmas windows, and soon strollers down Broadway could 'read' a series of stories as they passed each window: dolls sight-seeing at Niagara Falls (with real water); 'Charity', with a well-dressed doll handing a coin to a street-sweeper doll. In Germany, the two Sundays before Christmas were named Silver and Golden Sunday, when Sunday-trading restrictions were lifted, and foot traffic increased. (A third, Copper Sunday, was added later in response to retailers' demands.) In England, the word 'Christmas' had come to mean decorative greenery; by the 1890s in the USA, it meant to go shopping for Christmas presents, or, in cities, to look at the shop windows – 'with the children [to] Macy's to see "Christmas"'.

Even the most austere New England families did not remain immune. The poet Emily Dickinson remembered her childlike 'transports' brought on by the idea of Santa Claus and his sack. By the end of the century, even those on the fringes of society expected presents: in one magazine story a trapper living in the wild receives a box and automatically assumes 'it be a Christmas gift'. Of course, the author probably had no intimate acquaintanceship with fur trappers – it was more likely that by now middle-class expectations were so ingrained as to be automatic in writer and readers both. What is not imaginary was the sense of entitlement with which many in the middle-class received their gifts. A schoolgirl in Rochester, New York, in 1898 summarized her haul: 'I don't think there is any use

writing down all the things given me but just say that . . .
I had everything I wanted except my gold watch' – that
is, the only gift she wrote down was the one she didn't
receive. Another teenager did list everything, but added
despondently: 'In all, I got 30 [presents]. Marie Van L. got
over 70.'

Expectations of gifts, and their prominent advertising
and displays, were indicative of another facet of gift-giving.
It was not the gift alone, nor the giver and the recipient,
that mattered. The ceremony of giving, the structure and
the shape of the handover, meant as much, and perhaps
more, than the object. In 1798, when Coleridge described
that north German Christmas, the children kept their siblings' presents hidden so as not to spoil the surprise before
the ceremonial moment. This tells us that the presents
were not wrapped. In 1848, too, in the famous engraving
of Victoria and Albert's tree, the presents underneath are
entirely visible: model soldiers, including one that might be
in Roman dress, a train and a doll's house. More presents
hang on the tree, some tied to the branches, others set in
little baskets.

Decorations on trees in Germany were part decorative, part gift – they were attractive, and then they could
be handed out and eaten. In Switzerland, *Samichlaus-Züg*,
or 'Santa-stuff', included fruit, both fresh and dried, nuts,
biscuits in the shape of animals, *Tirggel*, which were biscuits shaped in a mould and then decorated, and *Lebkuchen*,
a widely popular honey, nut and spice biscuit. Other
German tree ornaments included marzipan moulded
and painted to resemble animals: squirrels holding nuts in
their paws, a rabbit munching a marzipan cabbage-leaf.
The Pennsylvania Germans favoured marzipan and also

Matzebaum, almond-paste biscuits impressed with the outlines of animals, birds or flowers and then painted. During the Civil War, the soldiers had to make do, and the decorations of one German tree on the Union side included a soldier's biscuit ration cut into traditional Christmas shapes, interspersed with slices of salt pork or beef.

Where edible gifts could not be strung up by themselves, they were displayed in various types of holders, such as the 'gilded egg cups, [and] paper cornucopiae' found on the tree of a German professor at Harvard in 1832. A cornucopia was, at its simplest, a piece of paper or cardboard rolled into a cone shape and filled with sweets, or biscuits, or nuts, or dried fruit, then hung on the branches from a string. They could be made at home for barely any cost, and as the fashion for trees grew, shops sold fancier ready-made versions, printed with angels, or Santas, or embellished with decorative borders, or constructed from special papers. In the 1880s German-imported 'dresdens' came into fashion, embossed boxes of pressed cardboard, lacquered to look like polished metal, in shapes that included 'dogs, cats, suns, moons . . . frogs, turtles . . . a whole sea full of fish . . . a virtual zoo of exotic creatures, including polar bears, camels, storks, eagles and peacocks', as well as items from the modern world: bicycles, skates, sleds and ships. Unlike the cornucopias, dresdens were luxury items, many costing more than their contents: in 1882, golden dresdens shaped like angels cost a whopping 12¢ each.*

The shift from cornucopias to dresdens marked a shift

---

* For comparison, the Homestead Act passed the same year entitled western settlers to claim government land for homesteading at $1.25 per acre.

in presentation that was reflected in the gifts themselves. As we saw, the presents on that table in Windsor in 1848 were not wrapped, even in a royal household, just as baskets and cornucopias on trees displayed their contents. Dresdens, however, were closed, making their contents mysterious. And in those two decades between cornucopias and dresdens, presents, too, began to be covered up.

Early mentions of gift-wrapping are rare, and difficult to distinguish from the white or brown paper shops used to protect purchases on their journey home. In the 1860s a children's book published in Boston mentioned in passing the 'white papered presents' under the tree, as though everyone did it, yet Nast's 1863 engraving of Santa Claus in the army camp shows that the soldiers' gifts came unwrapped in their wooden shipping crates. As late as the 1880s a British children's book describing a German Christmas felt it needed to explain, as though it would not otherwise be understood: 'Every present is wrapped up in paper, and labelled from Mary to Jane, or Jane to Mary, as the case may be.'

The wrapped present, arriving in the middle of the nineteenth century, fits chronologically with the pervasive mid-Victorian approach to decoration more generally, one perhaps best described as Things to Put Things In and Things to Cover Things With. Partly this was a matter of taste, but coverings and boxes were also pragmatic responses to gas-lighting and coal fires. Gas was much brighter, and easier to use, than candles or lamps, but it had significant drawbacks: it damaged textiles and metals, and degraded dyes. It also left behind a sticky residue that settled on every surface; the soot from the coal then stuck to the residue, making endless daily cleaning both laborious and necessary. Hence the great Victorian cavalcade of containerization: glass jars to cover flowers and ornaments; cases for spectacles, handkerchiefs and watches; covers for matchboxes; bags or jars for tobacco; folders to hold blotting paper, or stationery, or stamps; embroidery covers, needle cases and pin cushions; bags for fabric scraps, or buttons; toilet-table covers; slipper bags, stocking bags, nightgown and lingerie bags and more.

As covering things became routine, so covering presents, never previously thought of, must have begun to appear natural. Other changes were also afoot, to make wrapping a present desirable. When only parents gave children presents, the items could be categorized as goods of either luxury or necessity. On the one hand, 'rocking horses, omnibuses, superior dolls elegantly dressed . . . magic lanterns, [marionettes], magical dancers, conjuring tricks, dinner and tea sets . . . archery bows and arrows'; on the other, socks, shirts, boots. Who would want to cover up the glory of the first with brown or white paper, and why would anyone bother with the latter? Similarly, when children began to give their parents or siblings presents, the gifts were handmade, and tended to be things to cover things: a spectacle case for father, an embroidered folder to put needles in for mother, a blotting-paper case for a brother going off to school. There was no point in covering up a thing intended to be a cover. Soon, however, the industrial revolution, and the reduced prices that followed the arrival of mass-produced goods, meant that children, too, could purchase gifts for their parents and siblings. These new gifts fit into none of the previous categories: they were not luxury goods (children rarely had enough money); they were not goods of utility (parents bought children new boots, not the reverse); nor were they now home-made. Yet purchasing a present felt cold when compared to the love expressed by the time and commitment that went into a handmade gift. Wrapping a gift, therefore, was a way of decontaminating it, both of marking that it had been removed from the world of the shop, and of associating care and the personal with otherwise mass-produced item.* Gift-wrapping made *this* embroidery hoop, indistinguishable from the others in a shop or catalogue, different from *that* embroidery hoop, purchased in the same shop or ordered from the same catalogue. Love and care were imprinted into commercial products via the selection of paper, the writing out of a label.

This personalization was made simpler as large factories replaced small manufacturers: to ensure safe shipping across the country, or across the globe, each item was encased in its own 'pasteboard box', something that had been unnecessary when manufacturing was local. Then, in the later part of the century, department stores encouraged manufacturers to use boxes for all goods, as they made it possible for dozens of irregularly shaped items to be stacked high in displays. The development of the parcel post, too, boosted the popularity of boxes: a reduced-price parcel service was instituted in Britain in 1883, the same year that Montgomery Ward's mail-order catalogue in the USA expanded to offer 10,000 items, eagerly purchased by the many thousands of customers living days away from any shops at all.

---

* That this is the function of gift wrap is reinforced by the recognition that today home-made gifts, usually food items, are barely ever wrapped, or just have a label or bow added. They don't need wrapping when their labour itself expresses the giver's affection.

Advancing technology also contributed to the wrapping fashion. Brilliantly coloured printed papers became more easily available as chromolithography, a method of printing in colour patented in the 1830s, became less expensive in the later decades of the century. Patterned, printed or decorated paper thus became economically viable as a disposable covering for a gift, rather than an expensive luxury to be cherished in its own right.

It also, therefore, became big business. In the USA the Dennison Manufacturing Company of Maine had made boxes for jewellers since the 1840s. In the 1870s the company imported tissue paper for retailers, and soon sold it directly to consumers via Sears, Roebuck's catalogue, later adding instruction booklets explaining how to gift-wrap parcels. Then they moved on to produce labels, ribbons and boxes printed with holly and mistletoe and, in 1908, what may have been the earliest seasonal gift wrap, also printed with holly. This could be bought individually, or in a 'Handy Box', which also contained glue, string and labels printed with holly leaves – everything a household needed to wrap presents.

Wrapping then developed in two directions, one commercial, one domestic. During World War I, a postcard salesman in Kansas City was no longer able to get hold of Dennison's 'gift dressings' to sell in his shop. He made do by buying up elegant French envelopes and carefully removing their printed linings to sell by the sheet. These were so popular that the next year he bundled them up in packs, and, after that, began to manufacture his own paper, labels and ribbons printed with motifs that had become standard on Christmas cards in the previous decades: holly, mistletoe, candles, stars, snow scenes, or with topical images, marketed with booklets that assured customers 'Your Packages Reflect Your Personality'. With the Depression, demand only increased: wrapping made inexpensive gifts appear more lavish. Technology made home-wrapping prettier, as new coloured and curled ribbons came on the market; then in 1932 it became easier, too, with the arrival of self-adhesive Scotch and Sellotape.

Christmas wrapping was also changing retailing. In the 1890s many retailers had taken over the nascent wrapping business: frazzled shoppers could have their gifts neatly wrapped when they bought them. A shop assistant recalled a more fundamental shift around the turn of the century. His small shop had sold out of its seasonal ranges, so the staff packaged up non-Christmas lines in boxes printed with holly, holly wrapping paper and holly tags, turning everyday items into gifts and creating a new market where one had previously not existed. Manufacturers were close behind, and soon a raft of household and personal goods, with no connection at all to the holiday, were sold in boxes printed with holly motifs and the printed outline of a label, with 'To —' and 'From —' on it, transforming into gifts ordinary items of use: kitchen goods like knives, products for babies, clothes, especially small items like underwear, stockings and collar studs, or other purchases that were expensive and personal – a dip-pen and an inkwell were for household use and rarely advertised seasonally, while fountain-pens, stalwarts of Christmas advertisements, were personal possessions.

And, as the presents hanging from, or under, the tree, grew more decorated, so too did the tree.

Chapter Eight

While modernity, and commercialism, hit Christmas hard, they didn't replace old traditions; they simply created new ways to interpret, and enjoy, them.

In Pennsylvania, the holiday's decorative focus remained on the Putz, which reached its apogee in the nineteenth century. Many houses had at least a small Putz: branches laid on a table, on which holy family figurines were posed. More complex Putzes incorporated subsidiary characters and scenes – angels, shepherds, the Flight into Egypt – or more elaborate scenery – 'lakes, caves, rivulets, waterfalls, crags, mountains, hills, fields, villages with lighted up churches, castles . . . houses and shelters' which, as the century progressed, could be mechanically operated. These Putzes could be enormous, taking over an entire room on platforms low enough that small children could view them and with the walls lined with evergreen branches, and sometimes hung with candles, fruit and biscuits, like a tree. Much of any Putz was home-made, handcrafted or foraged; the figurines might be carved at home, or collected over generations; the platform covered with rocks and tree stumps (placed upside down, their roots made excellent forests), and moss that had been collected in the autumn and kept cool and watered for months in the cellar.

Children were barred from the room while the Putz was laid out, before the great reveal on Christmas Eve, followed by open-house visiting, as families wandered from house to house to see the Putzes, the children welcomed with cookies and sweets. Many Putzes had a narrator, who explained the story being depicted. (In the twentieth century, where Putzes survived, recorded music or radio programmes were added to the same end.) While historians of the Putz state firmly that the nativity story was central, their accompanying descriptions indicate a more elastic approach: one Putz showed the surrounding neighbourhood as it would have been 'some three centuries ago', complete with 'a group of Indians . . . mining jasper'; another included a Mennonite family walking to church beside a local canal and industrial plant; yet another, in the 1870s, a mountain and lakeside scene, came complete with waterfall, lake, frogs and fishes, a barnyard with horses and cattle drinking from 'the tiniest running pump', that sat beside a working threshing machine and grist-mill. One Putz replicated an entire village and its inhabitants in paper – houses, churches, barns, shops, farm animals, dogs, horse and carts, and all the villagers, as well as a train going through a mountain tunnel.

Putzes were also used to raise money for good causes, as Christmas trees were. These trees had by now become commercial products: virtually all German and British households that had trees had purchased them; in America the proportion of households that obtained their tree outdoors was initially higher, but the custom was prevalent in urban environments by the 1840s.

After the trees had been bought, they then acted as a commodity to display other commodities. Particularly in the earlier parts of the nineteenth century, when presents were hung from their branches and decorations were edible, these items were removed from display on the tree's branches, just as items were removed from a shop cabinet and handed to the customers. Trees in the USA were often placed by a window overlooking the street, unconsciously echoing shop-window displays. Thus, when tree ornaments became available to purchase, it was a natural progression.

From the beginning, Germany was the leader in the manufacture of these ornaments. By the early eighteenth century the tin-mines of the Erzgebirge mountains, in Saxony, in south-eastern Germany, were almost exhausted. To eke out a living, the miners created handmade gifts for Christmas markets. These carved-wood nutcrackers, toys and decorations made in regional style soon became representative of German Christmas style more generally, along with the regional hand-blown glass ornaments (glass-blowing had been a local industry long before the mines began operating in the fourteenth century).

Different places had different specialities. In the early days, Nuremberg tinsmiths turned out punched decorative pieces, some with glass inserts in flower or geometric shapes, designed to reflect a tree's candles. These were followed by 'icicles', narrow strips of silver foil to hang over branches, and by wire ornaments in the shape of birds, flowers and stars. From Sebnitz, near Dresden, came metallic pieces covered in cotton wool, die-stamped in the shape of sleighs, nativity cradles, or rural motifs like cottages and wells with descending buckets, or, later, miniature Zeppelins, and dogs listening to gramophones. Mannheim produced celluloid (and highly flammable) miniature toys and dolls. In Thuringia, stuffed angels, or fairies, were given chromolithographed printed faces; the region also specialized in crepe-paper or celluloid cottages, icicles, and fruit- and vegetable-shaped hangings.

Angels for the top of the tree were first produced in Nuremberg, then in Sonneberg, both developing from local doll-manufacturing businesses. These had wax or china heads and papier-mâché bodies covered by gold-coloured dresses. Other tree-toppers were more fanciful: birds of paradise, glockenspiels, gold, glass or brass flowers. Stars were popular, representing the star of Bethlehem. So was the treetop, or point, a series of glass balls of diminishing size, finished off with a spike. But the most common was the angel, soon secularized into a fairy. In 1850 Harriet Beecher Stowe's mother made 'a little doll like a fairy in white with gilt spangles & a gilt band around her head & a star on her forehead & a long gilt wand with a star on the end & gause [sic] wings spangled with gold' for her tree.[*]

This was home-made, but when exactly commercial ornaments arrived in the USA remains open to question.

---

[*] This description makes clear how carefully memories of the holiday must be examined. Stowe's brother, Henry Ward Beecher, born in 1813, wrote that until he was thirty, 'Christmas was a foreign day . . . I knew there was such a time, because we had an Episcopal church in town, and I saw them dressing it with evergreens, and wondered what they were taking the woods in church for; but I got no satisfactory explanation.' And yet just seven years later, his mother, who one presumes was one of the adults who failed to explain the holiday to him, was making tree decorations. In a similar fashion, in 1860 a York newspaper reported that a tree that year was topped by an angel 'carved from wood a century ago by Louis Miller'. Miller was born in 1796, so either he had not made the ornament, or 'a century ago' was more a reflection of nostalgia of than reality.

Illustrations before the 1860s tend to show trees decorated with home-made ornaments, but this may be because people thought this was the way a tree ought to look, and was not necessarily the way it did look. In 1860, a Pennsylvania newspaper praised a charity tree decorated with *Matzebaum*, animal-shaped biscuits, for what it called its 'old-fashioned' delights, which suggests that other trees had more modern decorations. A children's book published shortly afterwards included a description of glass ornaments without explanation, the authors clearly assuming that their child readers knew them.

Old-fashioned Christmases were what everyone was supposed to want, even as magazines promoted new decorations. By the end of the 1860s *Harper's Bazaar* described manufactured tree decorations, including 'globes, fruits, and flowers of coloured glass, [and] bright tin reflectors', along with images of political figures, clowns, angels and more. In Germany books such as Hugo Elm's 1878 *Das goldene Weihnachtsbuch* (The Golden Christmas Book) pronounced, in Martha Stewart fashion, on what types of ornaments were stylish (and contained advertisements for such ornaments in the back): 'Essential', it told the socially aspirant reader, was a mixture of the home-made – apples and nuts, gilded pinecones, marzipan – and the purchased – chocolate, blown-glass globes, and ornaments shaped like fruit, tinsel, artificial flowers, ribbons and a banner printed with 'Glory to God in the Highest' draped across the tree like a particularly jaunty sash.

Among the purchased ornaments, glass globes, or *Kugeln*, were always the most common. Early on, these were hand-blown and hand-silvered; by the 1860s they were factory-manufactured, and available in a variety of colours and shapes. In 1880 the owner of a general store in Lancaster, Pennsylvania, was shown a line of German glass ornaments by an importer. Despite living and working in the heart of Christmas-tree country, he doubted their potential, and placed a small order only when guaranteed his money back if they didn't sell. 'With a great deal of indifference,' he recalled, 'I put them on my counters.' Two days later, the story goes, they had already sold out. His much larger order the following year was still insufficient to meet demand, and by 1890, when Mr Woolworth had become the owner of a chain of thirteen shops, he went to directly to the source: to Lauscha, in Thuringia, where he ordered nearly a quarter of a million blown-glass ornaments.

Lauscha continued to be the USA's main supplier of all glass tree-ornaments until World War I put a stop to the trade, but after the war it quickly regained its position. No other glass-blowing areas could break the hold of that single town, and so others diversified. Czech glassblowers specialized in ropes of small glass beads: made in alternating shapes and colours, with cut edges, they flashed and sparkled in a tree's candlelight, and had the added advantage that, unlike wax, paper and cotton ornaments, they didn't burn.

Fire was the great risk. For many, the Christmas tree's *raison d'être* was the first magical view of the tree and its lit candles in single breathtaking Christmas Eve revelation. In daily life, candles and open hearths made fires more of a hazard than today we remember. Candle-lit trees increased that hazard greatly, as each candle was wired or tied to a drying tree branch, its weight altering and tilting as the candle burnt down and wax drippings piled up.

A series of inventions and contrivances designed to hold each candle in place with greater stability appeared over the years, but a lit tree was never a safe tree. Many households lit their candles only once, on Christmas Eve, prudently keeping to hand water and a stick with a sponge on the end.

In 1882 the Edison Illuminating Company built the world's first electrical power station, lighting the 400 lamps of its eighty-two customers. Four months later a Christmas tree, unsurprisingly in the home of one of Edison's employees, blazed out with eighty red, white and blue electric bulbs. For non-employees, however, electric lighting was too geographically circumscribed, and far too expensive, to be more than a gimmick. When it was used, it tended to be for some form of public event – in 1891 a tree with electric lights was put up in the children's ward of a New York hospital and four years later the White House tree was lit by electricity. At the turn of the twentieth century, however, General Electric bought out the Edison Company, and soon an 'outfit', a string of '28 one-candle power miniature Edison lamps', could be purchased for $12. Few could afford these (a low-end kitchen range in the Sears, Roebuck catalogue that year cost $4.85). Fewer still had houses wired for electricity. But, as the accompanying brochure pointed out, 'Miniature incandescent lamps are perfectly adapted to Christmas tree lighting. The element of danger ever present with candles is entirely removed, as well as the inconvenience of grease, smoke, and dirt. The lamps are all lighted at once by the turning of a switch, will burn as long as desired without attention, and can be readily extinguished.' The market was there, and in 1903 Austrian-manufactured strings of lights, with bulbs shaped like fruit, flowers and animals, or snowmen, or Santas, were battery-powered, and could be used in houses without electricity. By the beginning of World War I, prices had dropped to an expensive, but no longer astronomical, $1.75. Many insurance companies refused to extend policies to houses that had candle-lit trees, making the move from open flames to electric bulbs pragmatic as well as desirable. By 1912, when a tree was erected in Madison Square Park, its electric light was pro-moted as 'typically modern and American'.

This twenty-metre tree, with its 1,200 lights, was certainly both American and modern, far from the nineteenth-century domestic ideal. Germany and the USA had seen some trees in public indoor spaces – church halls, Sunday schools, orphanages, hospitals – but these were a way of extending the benefits of middle-class domesticity to those unfortunates who were not able to enjoy them otherwise. In Germany, trees were erected in hospitals and army bases during the Franco-Prussian War of 1870–71, broadening familiarity with public trees. After German unification they became a symbol of the new nation, and also of the new industrial world, of the prod-ucts of industry, of items of household consumption that had once been luxuries, and were now within the reach of more of the population.

And many of those goods manifested themselves as items for children. Just as the public spaces where trees were placed were spaces for children, so too most con-sidered 'Christmas . . . to be the day peculiarly sacred to children', as the American feminist and journalist Mar-garet Fuller wrote. This is not to say that Christmas had entirely lost its carnivalesque, rowdy feel. It was more that, as with the tree and presents, those activities too were becoming commodities to be bought and sold.

For example, groups of young men, often workmen in the same trades, in effect self-created latter-day guilds, had annually roared around the streets of Philadelphia at Christmas, according to their many detractors, drinking and causing trouble, in particular coming into conflict with the more domesticated middle classes who observed the local custom of walking along the main streets on Christmas Day, nodding and bowing to their acquaintances as they passed. The newspapers were ostensibly on the side of the middle classes, tut-tutting over the dreadful behaviour of the working-class rowdies, yet the headlines of those very articles indicate a more ambivalent attitude: 'Christmas Gambols', 'Fun on Christmas Day', 'Christmas Sprees', 'Christmas Sport'. This may have been because the middle classes, too, participated in those sprees.

By the 1830s what had been rural belsnickling had, in the city, been transformed into costumed men with blacked-up faces marching with home-made instruments – drums, pots and kettles and other noise-makers, calling themselves 'fantasticals' or 'callithumpians'.* From the 1850s they also drew on militia parades, both mimicking and mocking them, taking pseudo-military names like the Strut-Some Guards. These working-class groups were held up and found wanting by others who did very much the

---

* Callithumpian was a word of some political significance. Originating, sometimes as gallithumpian, in the West Country in England, it denominated Jacobins or other radical protestors. The callithumpians also drew on the traditions of groups formed for economic and social protest, who frequently used disguise, including cross-dressing.

same thing. But the contrasting parade groups were organized not around trades, but through shared charitable aims, such as temperance, or civic institutions, such as firemen, and they were run by the men in power, not the workers. Their parades were designed to promote and enhance their own social and commercial eminence while dismissing, often violently, similar street performances by those from socially lower groups, or from those holding non-mainstream views: one 1840 volunteer militia parade was praised as 'A brilliantly dressed, well-disciplined, obedient network of young men from good families', even as a fife-and-drum troop with black participants was assaulted.

Because the organizers of these approved parades were leading businessmen and merchants, often holding civic office, their parades gradually gained an aura of official sanction. By 1 January 1901, no longer could just any Philadelphia group decide when and where and with whom to march. City officials had control, sponsorship and cash, a set route, and oversight of costumes and music. Parades were now not a means of self-expression or holiday enjoyment by the workers, but a commercial event for the entertainment of the middle classes. When one magazine proclaimed that 'Christmas is now pre-eminently the "home festival"', with New Year's Day the 'away-from-home festival', they were partially correct. It was just that public spaces, too, had come under middle-class control.

Thus, even as increasing numbers of books and magazines nostalgically hymned the revels of Christmases past, those revels were being altered. Only in their imaginations did these middle-class authors and their readers want Christmases filled with feasting and drinking, gambling and rowdyism. They wanted, as the future historian

Thomas Babington Macaulay put it in 1800, Christmases of 'domestic happiness, of social courtesy'.

To accomplish this, part of what had been more obviously adult entertainment was transformed into children's. Theatres, many of which had barely been places for middle-class women, much less children, now produced winter children's shows, and an entire genre, pantomime, based on fairytales, developed to cater to the juvenile middle-class consumer. This was a continuing trend: myths and legends were also adapted to the new child-centred nature of the day. In parts of Norway *haugkallar* were ancient farm protectors, spirits that had lurked near ancestral burial mounds (*haugr* was Old Norse for mound). From the eighteenth century *haugkallar* began to diminish in importance, to be replaced by *nisser*.* *Nisser* also guarded farms, but by the early nineteenth century they were domesticated: they lived in barns, ate porridge left out by the family and increasingly were depicted as child-sized. Soon these barn *nisser* were joined by *julenisser*, or Christmas elves, who brought presents for the family instead of playing pranks on them. In Sweden, household gremlins, *tomten*, who once had to be appeased, and had been singularly unattractive, with long noses and claws, were likewise tamed, turning into *jultomten*, Christmas gift-bringers dressed in sweet little hats and white clogs.† From burial mound to barn, from fearsome to mischievous, their path is comparable to that of St Nicholas.

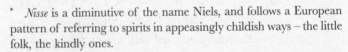

* *Nisse* is a diminutive of the name Niels, and follows a European pattern of referring to spirits in appeasingly childish ways – the little folk, the kindly ones.

† These gremlins are *tonttuja* in Finland, where they wear reindeer moccasins.

The shift in emphasis from adult to child was not merely socio-economic, or emotional. In part, Christmas took on its child-centred focus as adults very simply started to have less holiday time. For most of history, working hours were at the discretion of the employer, or the season, agricultural work having long fallow periods. Christmas proverbially came only once a year, but that didn't mean it came only for one day.* Industrialization had no cycle: it needed workers on a year-round basis. In Britain, paid holidays were at employers' discretion until the last third of the nineteenth century, and workers therefore disliked obligatory holidays. Scrooge famously refused Bob Cratchit more than a single day off, but it is unlikely that most clerks in Cratchit's position would have wanted more, as it would have been unpaid.†

From the sixth century Christmas had lasted twelve days, and continued to do so for those unconstrained by paid employment. Many in the nineteenth century, however, had no such luxury. A young man in Rhode Island wrote home to his family in the Midwest in 1851, wide-

---

* The origins of the proverb are cloudy. The playwrights John Webster and Thomas Dekker collaborated on a now lost play with that title in 1602, and, in the same year, Dekker used the phrase in his *Satiromastix*: '. . . you and your Itchy Poetry breake out like Christmas, but once a yeare'. Whether they, or one of them, came up with the phrase, or it was already in use, is unknown, although I have been unable to find any uses of it before that. It was however soon in common speech, and by 1659 it was included in a compilation of 'Proverbs, or, Old sayed sawes & adages'.

† Dickens may have seen an 1831 letter in *The Times*, when a labourer employed by an MP and banker applied to the magistrates when his Christmas Day holiday went unpaid. The magistrate regretted there was no law obliging payment, adding however that he thought the employer's behaviour was 'shabby'.

eyed: 'It would be hard to distinguish Christmas Eve, or Christmas Day, from any other day . . . here in Yankee land. The factories all run, stores are kept open all day . . . There is not that display of fire works, and fireing of pistols, and guns, that there is in Hoosierdom.' That same year, the whaling ship the *Pequod* set sail from Nantucket in search of the great white whale, Moby Dick, on Christmas Day: the whaling industry did not stop for holidays. (While *Moby-Dick* is fiction, Melville had sailed on a whaler in 1840.) In Britain, a rector in a Sussex village regularly married and buried parishioners on Christmas Day. Newspapers were printed and sold.[*] Other services were moderated, but not halted: by the 1840s the British postal service operated on a half-holiday basis on the 25th, reducing the number of deliveries from the usual twelve.

Many others were obliged to work substantial over-time. All of what we today call service industries were then the province of the hundreds of thousands of men and, mostly, women working as servants in private households. (By 1891 possibly as much as a third of the population of Britain was in service.) To provide the peaceful domestic Christmas of the middle-classes, phenomenal workloads were necessary for those who served them. With the arrival of the railways, many who previously had not been able to travel to see friends or family could afford both the fare and the time. Between 1861 and 1911 passenger numbers in England at Christmas increased in some places by over

---

[*] Many visitors to Britain today are bemused to find no news-papers printed on Christmas Day and, frequently, Boxing Day. Yet this is a tradition of the twemtieth century: *The Times* stopped publishing on Christmas Day only in 1913, and on Boxing Day in 1918.

500 per cent. Thus Christmas holiday gatherings, even with the smaller families of the later nineteenth century, could be large. To provide anything from half a dozen to two dozen people with four meals a day, to keep household fires burning, lamps lit, to carry water for two dozen people to wash, and to carry it away again, to keep clean two dozen chamber pots, was a never-ending task.

Compare the experience of Jane Carlyle, wife of the historian Thomas Carlyle, at a party in 1843:

> . . . it was the very most agreeable party that ever I was at in London . . . Only think of that excellent Dickens playing the conjuror for one whole hour – the best conjuror I ever saw . . . and Forster [a critic, and later Dickens's biographer] acting as his servant! – This part of the entertainment concluded with a plum pudding made out of raw flour raw eggs – all the raw usual ingredients – boiled in a gentleman's hat – and tumbled out reeking – all in one minute before the eyes of the astonished children, and astonished grown people! that trick – and his other of changing ladies pocket handkerchiefs into comfits – and a box full of bran into a box full of – a live-guinea-pig! would enable him to make a handsome subsistence let the book-seller trade go as it please! Then the dancing . . . the gigantic Thackeray &c &c all capering like Mænades!! . . . after supper when we were all madder than ever with the pulling of crackers, the drinking of champaign, and the making of speeches, a universal country dance was proposed – and Forster seizing me round the waist, whirled me into the thick of it – and MADE me

dance!! . . . Once I cried out 'oh for the love of Heaven let me go! you are going to dash my brains out against the folding doors'! to which he answered – (you can fancy the tone) – 'your brains! who cares about their brains here? let them go!' . . . when somebody looked her watch and exclaimed 'twelve o'clock'! Whereupon we all rushed to the cloakroom . . . Dickens took home Thacke[ra]y and Forster with him and his wife . . . to finish the night THERE!

with the behind-the-scenes record of the Christmas of Hannah Cullwick, a maid-of-all work in London at a slightly later date:

23 December 1863

I got up early & lighted the kitchen fire to get it up soon for the roasting – a turkey & eight fowls for tomorrow, being Christmas Eve, & forty people's expected & they're going to have a sort o' play. And so they are coming tonight to do it over & the Missis has order'd a hot supper for 15 people. Very busy indeed all day & worried too with the breakfast & the bells ringing so & such a deal to think about as well as work to do. I clean'd 2 pairs o' boots & the knives. Wash'd the breakfast things up. Clean'd the passage & shook the door mat. Got the dinner & clean'd away after, keeping the fire well up & minding the things what was roasting & basting 'em till I was nearly sick wi' the heat & smell . . . We got the supper by a 1/4 to ten, & we run up & downstairs to see some of the acting – just in the passage . . . We laid the kitchen cloth & had our supper & clean'd away after. I took

the ham & pudding up at 12 o'clock, made the fire up
& put another on & then to bed. Came down again
at 4 . . . The fire wanted stirring & more coals on &
when I'd got the pudding boiling again I went to bed
till after six. Got up & dressed myself then & clean'd
the tables & hearth & got the kettle boiling & so
began.

24 December

After breakfast I clean'd a pair o' boots & lighted the
fires upstairs. Swept & dusted the room & the hall.
Laid the cloth for breakfast & took it up when the bell
rang. Put the beef down to roast. Clean'd the knives.
Made the custards & mince pies – got the dinner up.
Clean'd away after & wash'd up in the scullery.
Clean'd the kitchen tables & hearth. Made the fire up
again & fill'd the kettle . . . We had supper in the
kitchen & then I dish'd up for the parlour. Lots o'
sweets came from Carter's & the jellies, & the man
dish'd 'em up. We went upstairs & stood in the dining
room door case & saw the acting in the other room.
Mr Saunderson . . . came & spoke to us servants &
was going to shake hands but I said, 'My hands are
dirty, sir.' . . . After supper was over the Master had
the hot mince pie up wi' a ring & sixpence in it – they
had good fun over it . . . We had no fun downstairs,
all was very busy till 4 o'clock & then to bed.

25 December

Got up at eight & lit the fires. Took the [carpet] up
& shook it & laid it down again in the dining room.
Rubb'd the furniture & put straight. Had my breakfast. Clean'd a pair o' boots. Wash'd the breakfast

things up & the dishes. Clean'd the front steps. Took the breakfast upstairs. Got the dinner & fill'd the scuttles. The family went up the Hill for the evening & I clean'd myself to go and see Ellen [her sister], but I'd such a headache & felt *so* tired & sleepy I sat in a chair & slept till five & then had tea & felt better . . . Had a little supper & home again & to bed at ten.

When Lord Halifax wrote, therefore, that on Christmas Eve his family 'used sometimes to practise self-denial for the benefit of the housemaids by not having a fire', it seems little enough, but no doubt the maids did feel the benefit. (Although note that carefully non-committal 'sometimes'.)

In the 1850s in Prussia, all work was legally banned on Christmas Eve and Christmas Day, and in some circumstances on 26 December, but the legislation specifically exempted domestic servants, and many more employers simply kept their workplaces open in defiance of the laws, in order that the Christmases of the middle-classes could proceed unhindered. In practice, it was places where the workers themselves went to enjoy their holidays – dance houses, bars, cabarets – that found themselves at risk of prosecution.

In the USA, after the Revolution, the holidays of the British calendar were expunged and no efforts were made to replace them nationally. By the first third of the nineteenth century, most people observed New Year's Day, the Fourth of July, Thanksgiving and Christmas. Thanksgiving was, however, regional, and religious, a day of prayer either of gratitude, or more specifically for deliverance from an epidemic, or famine, or war. It was often considered to be a local New England custom and, by many white

Southerners, something that abolitionists might favour. Yet it was Texas, in 1848, which first made Thanksgiving a state holiday, followed by more southern states before New England formally declared the day a holiday, prompted by a campaign by the formidable editor of *Godey's* magazine, Sarah Josepha Hale, herself a New Englander (and also, as it happens, the author of 'Mary Had a Little Lamb'). With the help of her campaign, and the impetus of the Civil War, it became a day dedicated to family, and domesticity, a day, in the words of President Grover Cleveland, of 'reunion of families . . . and . . . the social intercourse of friends'.

Chapter Nine

Looking backwards, it is too easy to assume the nineteenth century was a time of churchgoing, pious populations, careful of their interior religious lives, outwardly practising faith, hope and charity. A visit to the USA in 1831 assured Alexis de Tocqueville that 'there is no country in the whole world in which the Christian religion retains a greater influence over the souls of men than in America'. Modern Europeans have shared the views of their nineteenth-century forebears.

The figures, where they exist, tell a different story. In 1851 a census of religious attendance in England and Wales enumerated not the number of people of each denomination, nor how often they said they went to church, but the number of seats that were actually filled on one specific Sunday (Saturday for the synagogues). To the dismay of many, it emerged that just 60 per cent of the population went to church that day. Yet even that over-estimated church attendance: the census enumerated seats filled – anyone attending two services that day was counted twice. All that could safely be concluded was that between a third and half the population went to church on any given Sunday. These figures echo those for church atten-dance in the USA in the twentieth century: in 1939, 43 per cent of adults attended a weekly service; in 1998, it was 40 per cent.* The difference between being born into a religion, being a member of a congregation and actually attending a service were substantial.

Those, however, who considered themselves only nominally churchgoing nevertheless frequently sent their children to Sunday schools, becoming wholehearted participants in the new child-centred domestic customs of the holiday. Tree decoration and visits from the gift-bringer – the Christkind, Father Christmas or Santa Claus – were approved of by the clergy, as gifts on Christmas Day drew the focus towards the religious holiday and away from the secular New Year's Day. The evangelical movement also promoted children's services on Christmas Day: the Congregationalist minister Alexander Fletcher, dubbed 'The Children's Friend', famously held Christmas Day services for, in 1827, over 4,000 children from twenty-eight Sunday schools at his north London chapel.

More common still was a focus on charitable acts around the holiday. From at least the eighteenth century in England, prisoners had received extra rations of beef, beer and bread on the day with, sometimes, coals for their fires, usually given in the name of a civic leader such as a mayor or sheriff, lending the increased rations an aura of

---

* Although, unlike the 1851 census, these US attendees self-reported, which might mean the figures are overstated. Figures for the USA in the twenty-first century hover around 37 per cent when self-reported, 22 per cent when assessed independently. Compared to Europe, however, even that latter figure is remarkable, the most religious countries in Europe (over 50 per cent in Malta and Poland, 46 per cent in Ireland) being outliers; few others rise into double figures.

patriarchal benevolence rather than, to peeved taxpayers, superfluous luxuries. This may be why, when the Poor Laws established workhouses in Britain as a place of last resort, even then extra meat was served on Christmas Day. Also often mentioned, but impossible to measure, were individual acts of seasonal charity, like that of the politician Lord Whitworth, a figurehead lieutenant-colonel to a local infantry regiment, who gave a Christmas dinner for all 700 soldiers. As the century progressed, charity became more closely tied to domesticity. The owners of J. & J. Colman, manufacturers of mustard, starch and laundry-blue (whitener), were devout non-conformists, and at Christmas each of their employees received a roasting joint for their Christmas dinner, the size dependent on the size of their family (carefully ascertained by Mrs Colman beforehand). Into the twentieth century, other factory owners also inaugurated Christmas parties for their employees' children, or teas, or other forms of domestic entertainment for families of work, rather than blood.

Thus the central elements of Christmas continued to be secular. Many writers paid token homage to the nativity, but when newspaper and magazines and books are assessed, far more space was occupied by the worldly and domestic contributions to the day. *The Book of Christmas* gave fifteen pages to preparations such as buying food and drink, and dispatched religion in ten lines. In the USA, there was both the token acknowledgement and the lack of space given to the subject. In 1858 the *San Antonio Herald* appeared to forget the Christian origin of the day altogether, wishing 'a happy Christmas to one and all whether Christian, Jew or Gentile . . . or of no denomination at all'. And that middle-class story of the backwoods trapper and his Christmas parcel cited in chapter 7 has him determined to keep the day 'as it orter be kept . . . we'll laugh, and eat, and be merry'.

If anything, religion was grafted on to consumerism, rather than consumerism grafted on to religion, and the increasing access to mass-market goods, and consequent increased focus on Santa and gifts as the core of the Christmas experience, made that seem entirely natural. A US trade card for a dry-goods shop in the 1870s has an illustration of two children kneeling in prayer, followed by a second one captioned 'Answer to prayer': the children opening their presents. In the accompanying poem, the children pray to 'Dear Jesus' to ask for a list of gifts before adding, dutifully, 'Bless papa, dear Jesus'.

In 1898 the windows of one of the major New York department stores displayed a church, some three metres long, and a metre and a half high, constructed entirely from handkerchiefs. From a church made out of commercial goods to a place of commerce turning itself into a church was a small step. The department store owner John Wanamaker was a lay minister and the founder of what became the largest Sunday school in the USA. After his flagship Wanamaker's department store in Philadelphia was rebuilt in 1911, its Great Court was decorated every Christmas as though it were a cathedral, with background music of recorded carols and hymns, and customers were handed a pamphlet of devotional texts: shopping with uplift.

Yet a look at a new tradition, the Christmas card, reinforces how little religion was in most people's minds. The first modern Christmas card was produced in Britain in 1843, two years after the creation of the penny post. It cannot be coincidence that the assistant to the mastermind behind the penny post was also the man who commissioned the first Christmas card: Henry Cole.* The card's centre illustration shows three generations of a family around a holiday table, toasting the absent friend of the caption, while two subsidiary panels show charitable giving. Each card was hand-coloured, and sold for a very expensive 1s.. They were not a commercial success, but others followed.

The first card in the USA was printed around 1850, and showed Santa with gifts, a party and a family opening their presents. Unlike Cole's card, it was monochrome, and there was no holiday message, just 'Pease's Great Varety [sic] Store in the Temple of Fancy': it was a trade card for a shop. The cards that followed were in a similar mould, trade cards that added seasonal images under phrases like 'Joy!' and 'Mirth!' It was 1875 when Louis Prang, a German immigrant who had built up one of the largest art-printing businesses in the country, produced the first American card to include printed Christmas wishes. Prang became the most successful Christmas card printer in the US, exporting to Europe as well. He drew on his art background for images, as well as his expertise in chromolithography, and

* Henry Cole (1808–82) began as a clerk in the Parliamentary Record Commission, which he immediately, and publicly, exposed as a hotbed of sinecure and corruption. He then worked with Rowland Hill on his campaign to reform the postal service before beginning to campaign for railway reform, write children's books and produce a line of 'art manufactures', or paint-boxes, as well as designing an award-winning tea-service. He became the de facto administrator of the Great Exhibition of 1851, and was then appointed secretary to the government department charged with establishing training schools for art and design, and the new South Kensington Museum (later the Victoria and Albert Museum).

also indulged in the fashionable trends for embellishment, finishing his more expensive cards with tassels, fringes, lace, feathers or spangles. Some cards contained pamphlets printed with extracts from literature, or children's stories. Their size, and lavish finish, as well as the content made them gateway presents – gifts for people who, because they were not related by blood, or dependent on you, had not previously been given gifts.

What is striking for those who continue to believe Christmas was ever primarily a religious holiday is the lack of religious content across all cards in English-speaking markets from their earliest days. One historian has catalogued the subjects in a collection of over 100,000 cards printed before 1890. The majority showed holly, mistletoe and Christmas pudding, Father Christmas or Santa, Christmas trees, bells and robins, food and festivity.* Next in popularity came snow scenes, bells and, as a subcategory of the village snow scene, the occasional church steeple. On Prang's retirement towards the end of the century, German printers, who led the world in chromolithography,

---

* Why robins became a Christmas regular is unknown. It might be that the red breast links it chromatically to holly berries, or possibly the bird was a reference to hunting the wren, an old St Stephen's Day custom in parts of England and Ireland, when boys hung a dead wren from a stick and processed through their village reciting a verse:

> The wren, the wren, the king of all birds,
> St Stephen's Day was caught in the furze;
> Although he is little his family is great,
> I pray you, good landlady, give us a treat.

A simpler explanation might be that robins had earlier appeared on Valentine cards, their red breasts a symbol of the heart, and the image was unthinkingly transferred.

began to dominate the market. In their home market, their cards featured images of the holy family, or angels, or the Christkind, although very often these were included together the secular: a tree, presents, the Weihnachtsmann.

Everywhere, food and drink were popular subjects for cards – turkeys, geese and boars' heads, game, puddings, bottles and punch bowls; so too were family parties. In the 1870s anthropomorphic animals – animals dressed as people, or performing human activities – became fashionable. Always popular were scenes of imagined Christmases past: in medieval times, or Tudor, in country houses, on stagecoaches. German cards had alpine scenes, or villages, not necessarily in winter. Personalized Christmas cards, with photographs of the senders, were also available: one photography studio in Dundee, Scotland advertised 'Christmas Card Portraits' at 6s. per dozen in the 1860s. The advertisement gave no explanation, which suggests the newspaper's readers already knew what they were. Yet even when photography made possible the reproduction of paintings of the nativity, cards with religious images remained what two historians of the subject have called 'very rare' or even 'insignificant' in number.*

 Christmas crackers preceded the arrival of Christmas cards by a few years, immediately becoming an instant new tradition. Tom Smith was a confectioner in Clerkenwell, an impoverished area of London. To distinguish his sweets, he wrapped them in paper treated with saltpetre, which made a bang as they were opened, calling them

---

* For those who feel 'Compliments of the Season' is a mealy-mouthed contemporary concession to the secular twenty-first century, the phrase was widely printed on cards from the 1860s.

'fire-cracker sweets'. Gradually, the sweet was replaced by a modest gift, the printed wrapper became a motto or joke and the Christmas cracker was born. Tom Smith & Co. became a dedicated cracker-manufacturer, and by the 1890s was producing 13 million crackers a year.

Another instant tradition, more prevalent in German-speaking lands, was the Advent wreath. The wreath was simply a formalized version of the greenery that had been in use for centuries, but with a candle in the centre as the focus of a ceremony it was the inspiration of a Lutheran clergyman, Johann Wichern, who ran an inner-city mission in Hamburg. From 1833, on every Sunday in Advent, he gathered the mission-school children to light a candle and retell the nativity story as a way of raising funds. The custom spread to homes, and churches and manufacturers began to produce commercial Advent wreaths, Advent candleholders and coloured candles.

While Advent Sunday ceremonies became known outside Germany only in the twentieth century, a later German Advent tradition moved more swiftly: the Advent calendar. Originally these were home-made calendars marking the days from the first Sunday in Advent to Christmas Day, sometimes with a Bible verse for each day. In Thomas Mann's novel *Buddenbrooks* (1901), which recounts the story of a north German family from the 1830s to the 1870s, the son of the house, little Johann, counts down to Christmas with 'the help of a calendar manufactured by [his nanny], with a Christmas tree on the last leaf'. Two years after the novel was published a Munich stationer produced the . first commercial Advent calendar, and soon these became mainstream, now beginning on 1 December rather than the first Sunday in Advent, so that stock could be carried over from one year to the next. These early calendars had a Bible verse, or a pretty scene for each day, which were soon covered by flaps or pull-outs. The calendars later became secular, with jokes or sweets and small toys, or comic and television characters hidden behind the flaps.

Other traditions took longer to move from their local origins. As the Christkind had consciously been created to replace the wild men of legend, so in north Europe was Santa Lucia. The third-century martyr had been blinded for her faith, and she was therefore the patron saint of light, bringing her gift to the darkest days of winter. In many parts of Scandinavia from the eighteenth century, on her saint's day, 13 December, she rode out with the star boys and, as one court case heard, 'other loose persons'. In the nineteenth century, the saint followed a pattern we can now recognize, and became more domesticated. Now the youngest girl in the household, dressed in white and with a wreath surmounted by candles on her head, greeted her family at first light with coffee and cakes. This moved in the early part of the century to Finland, with its large ethnic Swedish population, and later to other areas of Swedish emigration. Soon Swedish offices and shops were selecting a Lucia maiden; civic Lucia maidens represented their districts. The descendants, too, of other Scandinavian immigrants in the USA began to adopt the saint as well: in the 1950s, some Norwegian communities began to mark Lucia day.

These seemingly transplanted customs were often in reality freshly rooted. The emigrants themselves had frequently been eager to discard the trappings of the Old World, and it was their descendants who wanted to relearn, and reproduce, the traditions of previous generations. The

Swedish-American Vasa Order was founded in 1896 to promote Swedish culture in the USA, but it was 1962 before a town such as Lindeborg, Kansas, where two-thirds of the population were of Swedish descent, held Lucia Day ceremonies, and those were prompted by the town's chamber of commerce, to promote local shops.

Otherwise, in the Nordic countries, Christmas remained for much of the population a more public, communal festival devoted, once again, to food and drink. Foods varied from region to region, on the coasts often *lutfisk* (a preserved whitefish), elsewhere a fish soup; in many areas pork products, butchered specially for the holiday; other dishes were herring salad and rice soup or pudding. Baking was an essential component, and a table laid out with piles of cakes and breads was what marked the holiday. In Norway, the stress was on the *julebord*, the pre-Christmas-day spread, and the *koldtbord*, the Christmas morning cold buffet.

Straw, too, was a holiday marker in many Nordic areas. In earlier times, households slept on straw-strewn floors on Christmas Eve; straw figures, especially of the Christmas goat, were made; Christmas crowns, decorated straw hangings shaped like stars, or squares, or rectangles, hung from the ceiling. A Christmas sheaf, a sheaf of wheat, was placed outside. The origins of this custom are unknown: it was practised by the mid-eighteenth century, but whether it was a survival of older pagan traditions, possibly representing food for the dead, or a marker of charity in leaving food for the birds, is uncertain. The sheaf, however, continues to be reproduced routinely along with Christmas *nisser* on cards and holiday wrapping paper.

This was a standard pattern. Holiday traditions and symbols frequently originated with the economically deprived before being turned into products and mass produced, becoming commodities admired, sometimes across the world, as representative of authentic folk culture. Many more pastimes which could not be straightforwardly sold – they were ideas or events rather than objects – were commodified nonetheless by being included in books and magazines, sold as the practices of simple country-folk. The nineteenth century was particularly rich in antiquarianism, and therefore equally rich in these reformatted practices. Some had elements of genuine tradition clinging to them, many more seem to have been woven out of the most tenuous threads. And then there were always a few that were simply outright fabrications, intentional or otherwise. William Hone's *Every-Day Book* was a compilation of the editor's antiquarian reading, promising an outline of 'popular amusements, sports, ceremonies, manners, customs, and events . . . in past and present times'.

His report, therefore, of 'hodening', on the Isle of Thanet, where men processed a horse's jaw around the village, snapping its head at spectators, carefully notes that it was merely '*supposed* [my italics] to be an ancient relic' of 'our Saxon ancestors'.*

Other traditions were innovations. 'Stir-up Sunday' was so-called from the Church of England collect read on the last Sunday before Advent, which begins, 'Stir up, we

---

* Hone loses a little credibility by citing a comic anthology entitled *Busby's Concert Room and Orchestra Anecdotes* as his source. A twentieth-century folklore expert records the first surviving reference to the practice of hodening only to 1807. He adds dryly that any descriptions of traditions that include the words 'pagan', 'fertility' or 'Celt' are likely to be dubious, while those using 'sacrifice', 'Druid', 'earth goddess' or 'vegetation spirit' are 'complete nonsense'.

beseech thee, O Lord, the wills of thy faithful people'.
Today it is often claimed as the day Christmas puddings
have always been made. Instead of being long-established,
however, it was a clergyman at the end of the eighteenth
century who noted the phrase; it was repeated, with a little
verse, in a collection of folklore published in 1843: 'Stir-up,
we beseech thee, / The pudding in the pot: / And when
we get home, / We'll eat it all hot', although the book's
editor, another clergyman, considered the tradition 'profane'. After that, a few authors used the phrase to indicate
the date, with no mention of puddings; a few more used
it to mean the approach of the school holidays. It was only
in 1870 that the bestselling novelist Rhoda Broughton used
it in its current 'old' sense: '"Stir-up Sunday" is past;
people have bought their raisins and suet and citron', she
wrote as though it were a commonplace.

Less routine, but consistent over the course of the nineteenth century, were stories that attempted to pin ancient,
and usually aristocratic, origins on much more mundane
things. There was the Christmas joint of meat, said to
have been raised to gentry status when a loin of beef was
brought before (insert name of monarch here – Henry
VIII, James I and Charles II were favourites), who, 'in a
merry mood', proclaimed the beef so good, it was worthy
of knighthood, dubbing it 'Sir Loin'. (More prosaically,
Old French *surloigne* – 'over the loin' – indicates the location
of the joint.) Other newspaper stories regularly pulled
out that old favourite, mocking foreigners, especially the
exquisite comedy of their not knowing how to make a
Christmas pudding, when the [name of important for-
eigner here] gave his cook the ingredients for a Christmas
pudding, to honour a visiting Englishman, but it was served

as a semi-liquid mass for 'he had forgotten all about the cloth' (usually followed by an exclamation point). That one was retrospectively attributed to high-ranking dignitaries in China, as well as, closer to home, the French kings Henri IV and Louis IX.

Many other traditions were only partially fabricated. There were numerous New Year fire festivals, most of which were, at best, archaized. At Burghead, on Scotland's Moray Firth, burning tar barrels were rolled through the streets on 11 January, using the pre-1752-calendrically adjusted New Year's Day to indicate the supposed great age of the custom. Burghead, however, was founded only in the nineteenth century, so if this procession was older, it came from elsewhere. Similar is the Up-Helly Aa, in Lerwick, on Shetland, still celebrated today, and regularly described as having Viking origins, its curious name attributed to convoluted derivations from the Old Norse for 'festival'. In reality the first Up-Helly Aa was organized by a temperance society in the 1870s, to keep young men away from New Year drinking; its name is dialect for up-holiday (the holiday is up, as in over). Equally, when the Revd Francis Kilvert wrote in 1877 that Herefordshire locals practised 'the old custom of Burning the Bush on New Year's Day . . . the whole valley can be seen early on New Year's morning alight with [such] fires', he was, undoubtedly, recording what he was told, and what he saw. But there is no record of such fires before the 1850s, and by the early twentieth century their brief era had come and gone.

Meanwhile, in Scotland and the north of England, such mutations were changing the shape of the holiday altogether. Christmas had not officially been a holiday in Scotland from the seventeenth century, but actual practice depended on the location. The further away from the centre of government, the less likely the locals were to observe the ban. In the Outer Hebrides and the Shetlands the older, pre-seventeenth-century holiday – the long period of festivity, the special breads and cakes – had continued without a break. All the Kirk had achieved was entirely to remove religion from the day, and people had no trouble with that.

Closer to governmental eyes, many of the ways of marking the holiday simply moved to New Year's Eve and New Year's Day, days without religious significance, and therefore not under any interdict. In some places, events resembling wassailing occurred, as children went door to door asking for 'hogmanay', or 'hangmen' – meaning the usual food, drink or cash.* One observer recorded the verse they chanted:

> Tonight it is the New Year's Night, tomorrow is the day,
> And we are come for our right and for our ray,
> As we used to do in old King Harry's day.
> Sing, fellows, sing Hangman heigh!

The Merrie England reference of 'King Harry' suggests a nineteenth-century creation, and indeed the only pre-eighteenth-century reference to 'hogmanay' was as a small New Year's gift.

Other customs were novel, the best-known being 'first footing', when the luck of the household for the coming

---

* The *Oxford English Dictionary*, with some hesitation, finds the origin of 'hogmanay' in the Middle French word for new year. It also lists spellings that include hagmena, hagman heigh, hagnuna, hogmena, hagmana, hagmane, hagmonay, hoguemennay, hogmoney, hugmenay, hangmanay and many more.

year was set by the first person to step over the threshold on New Year's Day. As time went on, different places had different first-footing customs: women were considered generally unlucky; sometimes dark-haired men brought luck, in others it was blond men; or the visitors carried luck in with them by bringing a gift, or speaking a set phrase – 'May your hearth never grow cold', 'Please to let the new year in' – or circling the room in a specific direction.

Areas of Scottish immigration saw the integration of these practices to the resident populace. A schoolmaster as far south as Yorkshire recorded in 1827 that 'we were very careful to fetch something in before any thing was carried out, so that we stand a fair chance of being fortunate'. A few years later his wife was horrified when 'a *Girl* got herself into the Kitchen, but she was ordered off in a hurry, and might think herself happy to escape without a kicking for showing her *unlucky* face this morning'.*

It was perhaps not such a happy holiday for all.

---

* It was Scottish émigrés, too, who promoted the tradition of seeing the New Year in together outdoors, although this did not become popular outside Scotland until the 1920s, when many copied the pattern of standing outside the Tron Kirk on Edinburgh's High Street by congregating outside London's St Paul's. In the 1930s that moved to the more night-friendly, crowd-friendly Piccadilly, and then on to Trafalgar Square after World War II (possibly only coincidentally beside another church, St Martin-in-the-Fields). In the last few decades, the location has moved once more, down to the river where the fireworks can best be seen. In New York, the place to be until 1904 was Trinity Square, in Lower Manhattan, after which Times Square took over (see p. 179*n*).

Chapter Ten

For many, New Year was a time not to hope for luck in the coming twelve months, but to pray for it. In the 1740s a congregation of Bristol Methodists initiated 'watch-night services' of hymns, prayer and scripture readings at full moons, when the unlit streets could be safely navigated. Gradually these moved to New Year's Eve, becoming a time to reflect on past behaviour that had fallen short of the ideal, and commit to future improvement. By the nineteenth century many other evangelical congregations had such services, both on New Year's Eve and now also on Christmas Eve. So too did High Church Anglicans: by mid-century, St Saviour's in Leeds, for example, held a midnight Eucharist on Christmas Eve, complete with three-metre tree and an elaborate nativity scene.

In Indiana Calvin Fletcher, who became a Methodist in 1829, at first did not pay much attention to these services. In 1830 his only new year thought was to wonder at the quiet: 'not a gun been fired no childrin running the street calling for New Years gifts &c.'. It was 1833/4 before he attended 'a meeting at the methodist church . . . to continue until the new year comes in'. While the phrase 'new year's resolution' does not appear in the *Oxford English Dictionary* until 1850, the concept was in practice before then.* Greville, in his memoir, summarized 1837:

> I wind up this year with this result: – I have led a very idle, unprofitable life, have read very little . . . and have been unhappy in consequence; but I have definitely resolved to give up the turf . . . With hopes rather than resolutions I will begin the next year, and with the conviction that it is never too late to turn over a new leaf.

More people, however, were like Calvin Fletcher, who was a regular chapelgoer, but was also drawn to the rowdier, more carnivalesque portions of the night. In Indiana, as elsewhere, shooting and explosions were key, having originally been introduced by non-British immigrant communities. At the beginning of the century, the commanders of the Lewis and Clark expedition took it for granted that this would be part of their men's Christmas. Lieutenant Clark wrote in his journal in 1803: 'I was wakened by a Christmas discharge found that Some of the party had got Drunk ['2 fought' he added, then struck through the phrase] the men frolicked and hunted all day . . .' In nineteenth-century Prussia, legislation banned shooting and other 'loud amusements' between 24 and 26 December. In Sweden 'shooting in Christmas' was traditional: the shooter crept up on his neighbours house, fired (in the

---

* Citations in the *Oxford English Dictionary*, which historically has relied on books rather than more topical newspapers and journals for its sources, can often be pre-dated, but in this particular case, it is not easy to find any citations before 1850, although that first usage, and the next example I can find, from the *Belfast News-Letter* in 1864, both use the phrase as though it were already well known.

air, presumably) and rushed off before he could be identified.

It is likely that German and Swedish immigrants took Christmas and New Year shooting to the USA with them, because it occurred in many regions where they migrated. The New World development was to shift from guns or gunpowder to fireworks, firecrackers and rockets.* Sometimes the newly arrived and the older residents encountered confusion as their traditions converged. A German in Houston in 1849 joined some 'Texians' on Christmas Eve, going house to house, firing guns and waking the neighbours. Although the custom of Christmas shooting was unknown there, once the residents understood that they weren't under attack, they welcomed the visitors, possibly because they had cleverly brought 'as much whisky as our saddlebags would hold'. One group commended their new German friend as he left: he was, he was told, one 'hell of a Dutchman'.[†]

Philadelphia residents enjoyed the mumming of England as well as the belsnickling of the Germans from the Rhineland, and some added Scandinavian 'Second

---

* The famous Times Square 'ball drop' was the brainchild of the son of German-Jewish immigrants to the Midwest. Adolf Ochs, the owner of the *New York Times*, had initially organized a German Midwestern fireworks displays for New Year, which drew the crowds away from Trinity Church. In 1907, however, Ochs settled on a novelty, adapting the old-fashioned maritime 'time-ball', a ball on a pole on the front of an observatory or other maritime station, which dropped at a predetermined hour every day.

[†] 'Dutch' meaning German was fairly standard, from 'Deutsch', as with the Pennsylvania Dutch, who were mostly immigrants from south-western Germany, the Alsace and the Moravians discussed earlier.

Christmas' celebrations, spending 26 December visiting after a quiet 25 December at home with immediate family. Their food, too, ranged from turkey and plum pudding to turkey and sauerkraut, a popular local combination. In the South and Southwest, southern European, especially Spanish, Epiphany bonfires met Mexican decorative festival lanterns, and migrated to Christmas Eve, as did bonfires in Louisiana and for miles along the Mississippi; in Texas and New Mexico they became *luminarias* and *farolitos*, little lights.

By the time the children of the first generations of immigrants were grown, the origins of many customs were no longer remembered, and to the next generation the holiday customs were not German, nor Dutch, nor Norwegian nor Spanish nor French; they were just theirs. The Norwegian-immigrant parents of the Wisconsin-born and Minnesota-raised economist Thorstein Veblen kept the holiday in Norwegian fashion, from Christmas Eve through Second Christmas to 'Thirteenth Christmas Day', but he and his siblings also received gifts of toys in the modern American style. Montana mining communities in the 1870s were made up of Montenegrin, Serbian, Albanian, Bulgarian, Ukrainian, Russian and Cornish workers: the Orthodox celebrated on 7 January; the Slavs' first Christmas Eve visitors scattered wheat and said, 'Christ is born'; the Cornish paraded house to house in costume, enjoyed wassail bowls and Yule logs and hung what sounds very much like a kissing bough.*

* Although some details seem more artistic than realistic: we are told visitors to the Slavic households kissed one of three logs in the fireplace, but it is hard to imagine unlit fires in midwinter Montana.

As Christmas moved indoors and became more domestic, music remained one of the most important outdoor pastimes. In England in the sixteenth century and for part of the seventeenth, small groups of instrumentalists called 'waits' were employed by civic bodies to play in the street or at town events, their performances only gradually becoming confined to Christmas. In London, Westminster parish burgesses seasonally licensed bands of musicians called the 'Ancient Wakes' to play in the streets after midnight. Others, unlicensed, cheerfully joined in, and by the nineteenth century these midnight waits had created another pastime: complaining about seasonal music: 'disturbing the good easy people who have a mind to enjoy sleep', a Yorkshire schoolmaster growled in his diary in 1826, before, he went on, those 'same disturbers have the impudence to beg of the Inhabitants to reward them, for undertaking to keep them awake'.

But in most places, such nocturnal music was welcomed. Despite the renewal of carol-writing in Britain in the eighteenth century, the middle and upper classes rarely encountered the genre, at most serenaded by a village group once a year. Even then, as Oliver Goldsmith wrote in *The Vicar of Wakefield* (1761/2), this was largely a characteristic of remote districts, where the residents 'retained the primaeval simplicity of manners', indicated by their '[keeping] up the Christmas carol'.

That was not the case in Germany, where the carol tradition had always been stronger than in English-speaking countries, and in 1818 developed further with one of the most famous German carols, 'O du fröliche', followed two years later by 'Stille Nacht, heilige Nacht' (translated into English as 'Silent Night' in 1859, and before and since into more than a hundred languages).* Both of these referred at least nominally to the nativity, whereas the equally popular carols 'O Tannenbaum', given new verses in 1824, and 'Morgen kommt der Weihnachtsmann' ('Tomorrow the *Weihnachtsmann* is coming') were about trees, toys and more toys.

In England in 1822 Davies Gilbert, an MP and anti-quarian with a special interest in the history of Cornwall, published *Some Ancient Christmas Carols, with the Tunes to which They were Formerly Sung in the West of England*. This was not the first English carol collection – there had been many cheap reprints and broadside collections – but it was the first intended for prosperous middle-class readers, the first to bring carols into respectable domestic and ecclesi-astical life, unlike broadsides, 'written by superstitious and illiterate persons' and thus dismissed. Gilbert included just eight carols; a second edition the following year added another eleven (of which only 'The First Noel' is still regularly sung). The book's significance was not in what it contained, but in how it was viewed. Gilbert, like many

---

* As with so many popular Christmas events, there's a perfectly charming and entirely fabricated history attached to this carol. The story goes that the church organ in the small town of Oberndorf fell into disrepair just before the all-important Christmas services, and so the curate (Joseph Morh, words) and the assistant organist (Franz Xaver Gruber, music) hastily cobbled together a carol to a guitar accompaniment. In reality, the church's organ continued to give good service for some years after the carol's appearance. More prosaically, the piece was heard by a visiting folk-music enthusiast who included it, as an 'authentic' Tyrolean song in a concert staged in Leipzig in 1823. A music publisher heard it there and published it as a traditional piece, and it took some time before the original authorship was determined.

scholars of his day, and Oliver Goldsmith before him, thought of carols as what *The Times* referred to as 'specimens of times now passed away', treasures that had to be 'made safe' and preserved as a record of a defunct tradition. William Sandys gathered his *Christmas Carols, Ancient and Modern* (1833) with similar intentions, but unlike Gilbert's collection, Sandys included many that are still heard: 'The First Noel', 'God Rest You Merry, Gentlemen', 'The Boar's Head Carol', 'Tomorrow Shall be My Dancing Day', 'I Saw Three Ships', 'Hark the Herald Angels Sing'.

In 1826 William Hone's popular *Every-Day Book* introduced carols to his middle-class readers as though they were entirely unknown. After giving a complicated (and entirely incorrect) derivation of the word carol itself, he gestured towards an ecclesiastical history: 'Anciently, bishops carolled at Christmas amongst their clergy', but, he added hastily, he would confine himself to 'domestic usages' of the form. In reality he had to, for there was only an extremely limited ecclesiastical history: the carol was a secular and demotic form. But that did not confer the respectability and gravitas Hone and other antiquarians desired. And so Hone took what was a fairly recent tradition and constructed a history for it; took what was secular and made it religious; and, most importantly, took what was working class and of the street and made it middle-class and of the hearth and home. He was followed in this by collectors over the following decades, who rejected popular carols as being 'deficient of interest to a refined ear', 'the veriest trash' and against all 'morality and good taste'. Sandys had acknowledged in passing that carols had survived in broadsides from London and Birmingham and a vaguely gestured-to 'other places' – that is cities – yet his antiquarian sensibility urged him to find their origins in the imaginary pastoral of Merrie England, more authentic somehow than the gritty reality of the proto-industrialized cities where carols had flourished. For the same reasons, African-American spirituals of the nineteenth century, such as 'Go Tell it on the Mountain', had to await the twentieth century to be valued by mainstream culture.

One way of taming these urban, working-class, secular songs was to incorporate them into church services. The rise in Britain of High Church Anglicanism, with its love of ritual and ceremonial, encouraged the development of choral singing, and smaller, less organized groups were replaced by what might be called corporate choral performances in which hymns were now interspersed with demotic carols. Soon there was no sense that these latter had only recently been introduced into churches. In 1872 R. R. Chope's *Carols for the Use in Church* blandly stated that it had been a 'prolonged and costly' job 'to *restore* [my italics] the use of Carols in Divine Service'. The book also happily rewrote history by stating that carols had been 'commonly sung in churches' in the eighteenth century (using as proof, oddly, the sentence from *The Vicar of Wakefield* cited above, which says exactly the opposite). At St Saviour's, Leeds, the midnight service on Christmas Eve was prefaced by what the curate himself referred to as a 'hymn' – 'O Come All Ye Faithful'.* To feed this new

* This attitude persists. In 1992, the otherwise entirely admirable editors of the *New Oxford Book of Carols*, despite their enormous knowledge of secular carols, treat religious carols as the template, with 'tedious catalogues of eating and swilling' the aberration.

enthusiasm for religious seasonal songs, churchmen (and a few women) now began to write dozens of new carols: 'Once in Royal David's City', with words by the wife of the Primate of Ireland; 'We Three Kings of Orient Are', by a rector from Pennsylvania; 'Away in a Manger', words possibly by a Pennsylvania Lutheran; 'It Came Upon a Midnight Clear', words by a Unitarian minister from Massachusetts, music by a church organist; 'O Little Town of Bethlehem', words by an Episcopalian minister.

Other carols had more unexpected sources. 'Hark the Herald Angels Sing' had music adapted from Mendelssohn, born into a Jewish family, although baptized as a child; 'Cantique de Noël' (the English version is 'O Holy Night') was set to music by the Jewish composer Adolphe Adam. The entirely secular 'Jingle Bells' was composed in 1857 by a church organist, James Pierpont, but based on the chorus of a minstrel song by Stephen Foster.*

This popularizing of carols was highly successful, and not long after the publication of Sandys' collection, carols were discussed as though they had always existed, and always been popular. A man remembering his Hampshire childhood in the 1860s recalled that they sang 'the *ancient* carols of England' (my italics), including 'O Come All Ye Faithful', which had been translated into English just twenty years before. In 1903 one magazine commended Oxford University for keeping alive its 'ancient'

---

* Stephen Foster (1826–64) was called the 'father of American music', writing over 200 parlour and minstrel songs, including 'My Old Kentucky Home', 'Jeanie with the Light-brown Hair', 'O! Susannah!', 'Camptown Races', 'The Old Folks at Home (Swanee River)' and 'Beautiful Dreamer'.

carol service, complete with Christmas tree and selections from the *Messiah*: three customs, none of which dated back more than 110 years, now all 'ancient'. So swiftly were new traditions made old, and yet given new life.

As all these customs – sacred and secular, Christian and Jewish, white and African-American – grafted on to each other, so too the ways the days of Christmas were spent also became, in the USA, a hybrid of the many backgrounds of the population. How the holiday was observed, therefore, varied by location and population.

The South and Southwest were the regions of American Christmas partying. Food, often shared communally, was of great importance, and drink was more so. Throughout the century, many drinking saloons, taverns and inns 'treat[ed] friends and patrons' to free alcohol on the day. Joel Chandler Harris, whose Uncle Remus stories made him famous, set a different type of story in mountain country during the Civil War. The meal, an attempt to 'remind them of the old days of peace and prosperity', was described as a 'genuine Christmas dinner': apple dumplings, chicken pie, barbecued shote (a young pig) and mutton and turkey. There was also, as a centrepiece, a large bowl of eggnog. One woman fretted about the latter, but was reassured it would be fine 'ef it's got Christmas enough in it, an' I reckon it is, kaze I poured it in myself' – 'Christmas' here seeming to be a synonym for alcohol.

Eggnog was virtually the national drink in December. When Texas became a republic, Sam Houston, the new president, warned on 25 December 1836 that 'only by continued sobriety and endeavor can a worthy republic be formed', a speech immediately followed by dancing and eggnog – apparently sobriety was relative, not absolute, on Christmas Day.*

The young John Pierpont, later a leading abolitionist, saw southern seasonal drinking at first hand when, as a young man, he tutored the children of a South Carolina planter.† The two or three days of holiday given to the slaves, he wrote, alleviated 'the miseries of the year' in 'hilarity and festivity' as they visited, ate the holiday meat ordered by their master, and danced and sang in 'a scene which might more than compare with the bachannal [sic] feasts and amusements in antiquity'. Their enjoyment, however, was owing to 'Rum, sugar, & water . . . prepared in large tubs of 2 or 3 pailfulls, and carried about them so that each one might drink his fill.' As the escaped slave and abolitionist leader Frederick Douglass described it, Christmas was a way for slave-owners to keep a lid on 'the spirit of insurrection': licensed drinking and hilarity for three days out of 365 was mandatory, and 'Not to be drunk during the holidays was disgraceful.'

Later in the century, the emphasis shifted from adult entertainment to focus increasingly on slave children, just as it had to their owners' children. Masters sometimes gave out presents dressed as Santa Claus, and the slave children might be invited to the 'Big House' to see the tree or hang their stockings. For the masters, however, these

---

* And nineteenth-century eggnog was a force to be reckoned with. One recipe recommended half a pint of brandy and a pint of Madeira (852 ml of alcohol in total) to every pint (568 ml) of milk. By comparison, the proportions in one modern recipe are 175 ml of alcohol to 940 ml of dairy.

† He was the brother of James 'Jingle Bells' Pierpont, p. 185, and both were the future uncles of the banker J. P. Morgan.

were incidental details in their southern Christmas, which was all about hospitality, parties and entertainment. The patriarchal arrangement of Irving's Bracebridge Hall stories was regarded as a model, the benevolent squire transformed into benevolent plantation-owner, the happy villagers into happy slaves. But the reality was rowdier, and vastly less sober. Everyone drank: men, women and children all, starting with a stiff eggnog at breakfast and continuing late into the night. And, as the tales of the great open houses of Merrie England masked a more nuanced economic story, so the daughter of a Mississippi planter remembered that, on the one hand, her parents issued no invitations because 'everybody was [just] expected', while, on the other, she clarified that one night was for entertaining former overseers, another for 'plain neighbours'.

In the North, too, drinking was part of the holiday, but there was already a separation between them and us, between the young men out in the street drinking and making noise and the more decorous family men with women and children at home. The changing holiday can be catalogued in the letters of John Pintard, written between 1816 and 1833. In the early years he wrote about New Year's Eve and its 'Bands o [sic] music, Bagpipes, Drums & fifes, boys bells &c. . . . till day light', while his family marked Christmas Day only by a toast to his absent daughter and her family, from 'your parents and Sister at their tranquil board'. By 1831 his Christmas Day was all about stockings, Santa and mince pies.

Canadian North America saw similar changes. In the maritime regions, with its Francophone Acadian population, the Old World tradition held sway: the single reference to Christmas in one New Brunswick newspaper as late as 1867 was to midnight Mass; there were no advertisements for Christmas gifts, and when the paper finally began to use the phrase 'Merry Christmas' it did so in English, stressing its foreign nature. The *réveillon*, when family and friends gathered, was held as a party in Quebec, with singing and dancing as well as food; or as a more modest family gathering after midnight Mass in the Maritime provinces on the Atlantic. In south-eastern New Brunswick the Christmas dish *poutine râpée*, pork-filled potato dumplings, was, despite its name, in origin a German *Knödel*, transported to Canada by Pennsylvania settlers in the late eighteenth century. Areas with some English populations adopted the plum pudding, renaming it *poutine en sac*, or *poutine aux raisins*.* In western France, Mi-Carême had been an old woman who handed out sweets to good children in Lent (her name means 'Mid-Lent'); by the nineteenth century in the Maritimes she had become the bearer of Christmas gifts, keeping Santa at bay until the very end of the century.

Mi-Carême at least merely moved her gifts from one Christian holiday to another; in the USA, such was the overwhelming presence of Christmas that other religions began either to take part, or create their own counter-holidays. In 1877 the *Philadelphia Times* reported that 'The Hebrew brethren did not keep aloof. Christmas trees bloomed in many of their homes and the little ones of Israel were as happy over them as Christian children. One

---

* The modern Québécoise dish of French fries, gravy and curd cheese named *poutine* appeared only in the later twentieth century. The origin of the word itself has variously been found in the English 'pudding', the Provençal for 'bad stew' and the Languedocien for 'a mixture', as well as a variety of other dialect words.

of them said: "Oh, we have the trees because other people do."' 'Other people' became an important motivator. The Jewish holiday of Chanukah had always been a minor one.* It was not coincidental that Chanukah began to gain a more public, more secular profile, first in the USA in the late nineteenth century, as Christmas trees became widespread. German Jews in America had seen Christmas trees back home, but to Russian and Polish Jews these new objects were emblems of the America they wanted to become part of, barely a matter of religion at all. Thus Jewish theologians and educators began in the 1870s to build new traditions around this previously overlooked holiday. Jewish Hebrew-school classes laid emphasis on the story as their Christian counterparts did on the nativity; Jewish children learned Chanukah songs, as their Christian counterparts sang carols; they lit candles set in menorahs nightly for eight nights as their Christian friends decorated their trees with candles; and they received gifts on their own holiday of 'Family gatherings, merry making, presents, feasting the poor and giving the little ones a good time'. That Chanukah's prominence was, and continues to be, reactive, a response to Christmas, is confirmed by the

---

* The historical background was a revolt in the second century BC, after the Seleucid ruler, Antiochus IV Epiphanes, had ordered a temple to Zeus to be erected over the remains of the Temple in Jerusalem, the holiest site in Judaism. Yehuda HaMacabee (Judas Maccabeus, or Judah the Hammer), with his four brothers, led a rebellion, and by 165 BC the Seleucids had been routed. To rededicate the Temple, oil that had been declared pure by the high priest was needed. Only one jar could be found, enough to burn for a single day, and yet, miraculously, the flames continued to burn for eight days, until more pure oil could be found. An eight-day festival of lights was the result.

fact that today in Israel it remains a secondary holiday, while in the USA, like Christmas, it is more commonly celebrated by Jews with children, and among secular or Reformed Jews, who are integrated into secular or Christian communities.

Dreidels, children's Chanukah toys, are prime examples of this type of assimilation. These four-sided spinning tops were originally Anglo-Irish, and known as teetotums. They had letters printed on each side: T for 'take', H for 'half', P for 'put down', and N for 'nothing'. A gambler spun the teetotum and the side that ended face up represented their winnings. Teetotums became popular in Germany, both for adult gamblers and as children's toys. In the USA, the Hebrew initials of a sentence that summarized the holiday, *Ness Gadol Haya Sham*, 'A great miracle took place there', replaced the gambling letters, and holiday games were constructed to fit.

By the early decades of the twentieth century American newspapers carried advertisements for Chanukah presents and Chanukah food (fried foods more generally, *latkes*, potato pancakes, more particularly, were traditional, as a symbol of the sacred oil). Aunt Jemima pancake flour promised it was 'the best flour for latkes', while Crisco shortening combined 'Hanukkah tastes and Modern Science'. As with Christmas, decorations could be store-bought or home-made: pipe-cleaner stars, paper chains of menorah or dreidel shapes. Magazines advised on holiday recipes (a salad of cottage cheese and fruit moulded into the shape of a menorah sounds particularly memorable).

Even as traditions in the USA drew from a range of cultures, so the Christmas of Britain was cohering. Christmases that had been quite different – Jane Carlyle and

Hannah Cullwick's Christmases, both spent at parties, bore no resemblance to each other – began to mirror each other more closely. The rich and the poor, the upper and the working classes had different resources, and the time they had to devote to the holiday was different. But by the end of the nineteenth century, for the first time, their aims aligned. A child living on a small farm in Hampshire, the son of a London architect and the titled widow of a colonial governor and Irish landowner all had holidays that included meals of turkey or beef, mince pies and plum pudding; a tree, if not always at their house, then at school or at a friend's or neighbour's house, plus greenery and decorations; presents, often in stockings; carols, at home or at school treats or parties; and various incidentals such as crackers and cards.

The working poor, too, partook of as many of these established traditions as they could afford. Trees were a luxury that they could not aspire to, both because of the expense and because their living spaces were simply too small. But greenery, cotton-wool 'snow', paper chains hanging from the ceiling – some form of decoration was considered a minimum. And as early as the first two decades of the nineteenth century, Christmas preparations had occurred even in lodging houses, where lived those who could not afford to do more than rent day to day, or at best week to week. In the kitchen of one such lodging house, an ambitious resident prepared a Christmas dinner of 'a very fine turkey, a beautiful plum pudding, and a handsome piece of pickled-pork' in the communal copper more regularly used for laundry.

To feed all these people, high and low, butchers' Christmas displays resembled solid 'walls of fat beef [and] wildernesses of plucked turkeys', the meat transported by 'railroads groaning' with fowl and game. As the century rolled on, it was more than trains. It was steamships, it was refrigeration, it was modernity itself that delivered Christmas: the meal of Olde England was composed of beef from Argentina and Australia, turkeys from Europe and Canada; dried fruit from the Middle East; fresh fruit from all the ports of Europe, from the Canary Islands and the Azores, as well as Canada and the USA; nuts from Europe and from Turkey; puddings made with sherry and madeira from Spain, doused with brandy from France. These ingredients, and the meals they produced, became not English or European or American. They were just Christmas, an old holiday brought to each home by modernity.

Chapter Eleven

Modernity was to hit twentieth-century Christmas hard, transforming it – not beyond recognition, but using the new forms of film, television and radio to create new traditions, traditions that, just as others had before them, would immediately become old.

Perhaps the most important modern tradition was that Christmas was inviolable: whatever was happening in the world that was wrong, according to this new thinking, Christmas would bring it to a halt for a period of peace and companionship. This grew out of what became known as the Christmas truce, in the first winter of World War I.

War and the holiday had become entwined earlier in the century, when a newspaper campaign encouraged patriotic readers to send chocolates to British troops fighting in the Boer War. Such was the success of this venture that Princess Mary's Sailors' and Soldiers' Christmas Fund was established – headed symbolically by royalty, with government approval, but in reality privately funded – sending each serving man a box of cigarettes and tobacco (sweets for non-smokers), and a card 'from' the king. So great was public enthusiasm that at one point both rations and ammunition were held back to enable these gifts to be shipped. During World War I, German newspapers also promoted *Liebesgaben*. One typical image shows officers at the front receiving these 'gifts of love' in a tidy, dry, well-lit space carefully decked with Christmas cheer: a small tree placed atop a box of ammunition, a holly wreath hanging nearby. There is no mud, no rats, no lice, nor unburied dead.

The seeds of the truce may have been sown at Messines in Belgium, where in 1914 a Bavarian regiment was encamped in the ruins of a monastery. Some of the men set up trees in the building's bombed cellar and, on 23 December, hung Christmas lights along their trenches, where they could be seen by the opposing forces. In a separate incident on Christmas Eve, members of the British Royal Flying Corps dropped a Christmas pudding over the German lines at Lille, reciprocated with a bottle of rum from the Germans soon after. For the truce was not a single incident, in a single place. Instead, gradually, on Christmas Day 1914, the rank and file shared their views on the chance to call a temporary halt to the licensed slaughter that had by then been underway for nearly half a year. Behind one trench a sign offered 'YOU NO FIGHT, WE NO FIGHT'. Elsewhere men simply called 'Come over!' to replies of 'Come over yourself!' On the whole, it was generally the Germans who led the way. The German army was at that date militarily far more favourably placed, with much less to lose; and their trees and decorations provided their opponents with a visual reminder of the holiday. And then there were their carols.
On Christmas Eve a Saxon regiment sang carols and folksongs along a candle-lit trench, and as each candle was lit, the British cheered. 'Stille Nacht', 'O Tannenbaum' and 'O du fröliche' came from the Germans, while the

British responded with music-hall numbers, or traditional airs: 'The Boys of Bonnie Scotland', 'Where the Heather and the Bluebells Grow', 'We Are Fred Karno's Army' and 'My Little Grey Home in the West'. 'Good King Wenceslas' was sung, as was 'O Come All Ye Faithful' and 'The First Noel', but the British choices were far more secular than the Germans'.

Listening to singing, admiring Christmas lights in the dark, was one thing; in the cold light of day, actually breaching the physical gap between the front lines required greater daring, and took longer to occur. But gradually, trench by trench, in one location after another, especially along the Flanders front, men emerged from their positions to speak to those who, a day before, they had been doing their best to kill. An unspoken set of rules came into force: the dead could be collected; no attempts would be made to strengthen fortifications in areas that would otherwise have been under fire; and if a shot was heard, it would be taken as an act of aggression only if both sides agreed that it was one.

The main activity was sombre, not celebratory: the gathering of bodies from no man's land, where they had lain, putrefying, without hope of recovery. While there was more than one report of football matches played by the two sides, these were almost entirely secondhand, seen by a friend, rather than seen by the speaker. What did occur was fraternization, men exchanging small gifts of food and drink, swapping badges, buttons or flashes from their uniforms as souvenirs. Boxing Day saw more of the same, despite the unease of commanders on both sides, worried that present friendliness would inhibit future bloodshed, or that concepts of patriotic sacrifice and duty would be nullified by exposure to basic humanity. Christmas spirit for those in command was treason. And so the fighting resumed, although on occasion preceded by a warning from one side to the other: 'Be on guard tomorrow. A general is coming to visit our position. For reasons of shame and honour, we shall have to fire.'

The truce lasted a day or two, and the generals ensured it was never repeated; its mystique, however, was felt for longer. As late as 1989 the BBC comedy series *Blackadder* simply assumed, correctly, that the elements of the truce – the carols, the football – were part of British general knowledge, and could be utilized without explanation. ('Remember the football match?' 'How could I forget? I was *never* offside!') Appropriately, the *Blackadder* sketch omits all mention of religion, which played as little a part in the truce as it has in the holiday itself over the years.

This can be seen, in a different way, in 1936, when the New York department store Lord and Taylor planned to accompany its Christmas window displays with recorded music. Religious music was rejected: 'This is Lord & Taylor's, not St Patrick's Cathedral.'* And by the 1950s,

---

* A compromise was reached in which a few carols were interspersed among more secular offerings. Yet it is not coincidental that the beginnings of what was later named the 'War on Christmas' by the religiously inclined concerned about the supposed increasing secularization of the day, has its origins in the period. Not, however, in commerce, or not directly, but in the writings of that notorious anti-Semite Henry Ford, whose 1921 book *The International Jew* warned of a devious Jewish plan to eradicate both Christmas and Easter. The fear was renewed in 1958 in a pamphlet, published by the right-wing Commie-bashing John Birch Society, entitled 'There Goes Christmas?!' (confirmation of the soundness of the rule, never trust anyone who uses double punctuation). The author's Cold War,

Wanamaker's, the department store that had for years turned itself into a proto-cathedral every December, was advertising 'Christmas isn't Christmas without a Day at Wanamaker's'. Instead, Christmas and department stores were, in the twentieth century, entwined in a wholly new way, as two holiday traditions – the Christmas of street entertainment and the Christmas of homes and children – came together.

Seasonal window displays became part of civic rather than commercial life, the unveiling accompanied by bands, speeches and perhaps a visit either from a local dignitary such as the mayor or from a celebrity. In the USA in the first half of the century, Christmas windows were crucial to advertising, their importance lessening only as growing suburban developments and out-of-town shopping centres reduced the passing foot trade. In Britain, Selfridge's windows in London's Oxford Street were initially the seasonal draw, but this was gradually transferred from a single shop to the street as a whole. As windows diminished in importance, 'turning on the Christmas lights' became a ritual community event. It always took place in a shopping street, yet somehow it was cleansed of its commercial origins.

Most of the subjects chosen for both window displays and lights were based on children's books or entertainment: circuses or giant doll's houses, tea-parties or picnics; *Little Women*, or *Alice in Wonderland*, Dr Seuss or Disney characters. Children were after all the main recipients of Christmas presents, and the commercial decision to look to the children was a sensible one. Or to the child in all of us,

---

Reds-under-the-beds paranoia was resurrected in the early twenty-first century, with the bad guys now the big-city liberals.

because most prominent in the displays was a sense of nostalgia, to evoke in adults memories of their own childhoods, or of simpler times, real or imagined.

Unlike the subjects on display in the windows, inside the stores Santa's Grotto, or Winter Wonderland, or the House of Santa, all maintained a single-minded focus on the gift-giver himself. While there had been variations on this idea from at least the 1880s, the promotional possibilities of a shop visit from Santa continued to expand, especially after shops moved to malls. In 1956 Dayton's department store in Minneapolis moved from its downtown location to a shopping centre, and its Christmas windows turned inwards, becoming decorations and displays that customers walked past as they entered the store. These were sometimes child-focused – one Baltimore department store reproduced a miniature version of Disneyland – but as frequently they were intended as a prompt to adult nostalgia: Dickens, or Grandma Moses, or Currier and Ives, or colonial-era displays.*

At their core, however, was Santa, by now firmly established as a red-suited, white-bearded man surrounded by elf-helpers who led the children, one by one, to share their Christmas-present hopes with Santa, while parents took photographs (or, later on, the elves did). The humourist David Sedaris describes his own experience, even if

---

* While the American printmakers Currier and Ives produced thousands of prints with a vast range of subjects between 1834 and 1895, today their name is used mainly to conjure up a vanished rural America. While that was certainly among their stock-in-trade, so too were current events: carnage on the battlefield, Lincoln's assassination – without question both entirely absent from twentieth-century department-store recreations.

heightened for comic purposes, working in the 1980s as an elf at Macy's in New York's Herald Square, where, he estimated, up to 22,000 people came through SantaLand daily, walking past 'ten thousand sparkling lights, false snow, train sets, bridges, decorated trees, mechanical penguins and bears, and really tall candy canes' to reach Santa's house. All of it was 'cozy and intimate, laden with toys. You exit Santa's house and are met with a line of cash registers'.

The commercial nature of SantaLand was obvious. By contrast, the new twentieth-century tradition of the pre-Christmas parade maintained a veneer of celebration and carnival. Today in North America, Macy's remains the most famous, and while its early planners referred to it internally as a 'Christmas parade', publicly it has always been Macy's Thanksgiving Day Parade, possibly precisely to remove this aura of the cash register from an event that marked the start of the Christmas shopping period. Macy's, however, was not the first department-store Christmas parade, nor was it an American innovation. Instead, the parade developed north of the border, originally in Toronto, at Eaton's chain of department stores.

Eaton's had been using Santa in its advertising from the 1890s; from 1903, their Toronto store had a visit from Santa each December. In 1905 an advertisement announced which train Santa would arrive on, inviting customers to meet him at the station. Such was the response that the following year the trip from the station to Eaton's was rendered more dramatic, with Santa in a carriage pulled by white horses and with four trumpeters alerting passers-by to the august visitor within. By 1911 the short trip from the station had come to take two entire days as it wound around the city under banners promoting

'Toyland at Eaton's', followed by store employees – and Eaton's owner – in procession. As the years rolled on, each parade offered something new to top the previous visit: reindeer from Lapland, a twenty-piece band, or floats carrying characters from nursery rhymes. One year Santa sat atop a giant fish (the reason for this, if there was one, is lost to history), on another, more comprehensibly, on an iceberg surrounded by polar bears. In 1919 Santa shunned the train for a more thrilling arrival by plane, which was filmed and screened in cinemas.

By now department stores in the USA were taking note. In 1920 Gimbel's in Philadelphia had already plugged into their city's nineteenth-century parade tradition by establishing its Christmas version, followed by Hudson's in Detroit a few years later. Then in 1924, Macy's hired Tony Sarg to dress their Christmas windows, which had long been famous for the mechanical ingenuity of their displays. Sarg was a puppeteer, the owner of a small show-cum-museum where marionettes performed a miniature adaptation of Dickens's *Old Curiosity Shop*. Under Sarg's direction, circus performers and animals together with shop employees marched from 145th Street to Macy's on 34th Street to drum up publicity for what was still considered the central component of the promotion, the big Christmas window reveal. Over the next few years, as the parade became ever-more elaborate, interest in the windows declined, especially after the introduction of giant balloon puppets that could be seen even from the back of a crowd.

Department-store window displays were static, and the consumer was a passive viewer: parades encouraged not merely spectating, but participation. In Winnipeg, 350 children competed in a talent show, vying for places in the Eaton's parade. In Montreal such was the community's engagement that by 1937 the Eaton's parade drew somewhere between a quarter and a third of the population. In 1952 the Toronto parade was televised and in 1959 Macy's once more followed suit. The cameras, unlike reporters on the ground, could not pick out the detail of the window displays, and so the parades became all-important. In towns and cities without department-store parades, community organizations – the Guides, Boy Scouts, Rotary and Lions Clubs – established their own parades in an echo of these more famous ones, heard about on the radio if not seen in cinemas or television.

Despite many parades' nominal association with Thanksgiving, their purpose was plain: in Macy's parade, the final float was always Santa's, marking the start of Christmas shopping.* Religious and patriotic groups complained about Macy's parade: the day, they protested, should be about religion and remembrance of the nation's history. Macy's bowed to pressure, rescheduling the parade in the afternoon, after church services and family meals. This timing, however, conflicted with the American football games that from the late nineteenth century had been played on Thanksgiving afternoon, and so the parade was swiftly returned to its morning slot – sport: 1, religion: 0.

These parades were but a faint echo of the earlier holiday street carnival, now ordered, given a purpose in the name of commerce, even as the commerce was covered

---

* Eaton's parades were always called Christmas parades: Canada's colder climate puts the Thanksgiving harvest holiday in October, not at the end of November.

with a thin patina of children's entertainment and patriotism. Merely scrape the patina, however, and the commodity market was visible. From its establishment in the nineteenth century, Thanksgiving had fallen on the final Thursday in November. In 1939 that was 31 November, compressing the run-up to Christmas into three weeks. A consortium of chambers of commerce and retailers campaigned to have the date made more shopping-friendly, and in 1941 it was officially established that henceforth Thanksgiving was to be on the fourth Thursday of November, which ensured it was never after 28 November, allowing at least four weeks of shopping.* The parades simply lent a vestige of drama to the exchange of cash.

So too did the US Christmas Clubs, which in more institutional form copied the older British goose clubs, or Christmas clubs, or coal clubs. Those had been informal arrangements, often centred on a pub, where people made small payments through the year in order to save for a Christmas luxury. In 1910 this idea was embraced by US banks: by 1912, more than 800 banks had joined in, and at the height of the Depression, more than 12 million people had a Christmas Club account. Christmas Club accounts were no different from savings accounts (except that they almost uniformly paid lower rates of interest), yet 10 per cent of the population thought it was worth keeping their Christmas money separately. Partly, no doubt, that was to ensure that the money was not spent on other items, or on emergencies; but part was that the separation – even the

* The change was mocked in *Holiday Inn*, a film made the following year, when at one point the camera pans to a calendar with all the holidays written in. When it reaches November, a turkey scrambles from one square to the next, unsure of where to roost.

lower interest rate – did for this commercial transaction what parades were doing for department stores, what gift-wrapping was doing for purchased gifts: bestowing on a commercial transaction an uncommercial aura.*

While the carnivalesque was thus being institutionalized, stray reminders of the old topsy-turvy traditions continued to survive in odd places. In the British army, to this day it is customary for senior officers to serve the Christmas meal to the junior ranks, as well as, in some regiments, waking them up with 'gunfire' (tea laced with rum – a twenty-first-century relic of both Christmas shooting and drinking). But this was the exception, not the rule. As we have seen, adults, in whatever position, were no longer the focus of Christmas; children were. And it had become women's work to manage the day. In the 1880s stories and magazine illustrations showed men bringing home presents, or organizing the Christmas turkey, as Scrooge had done for the Cratchit family forty years earlier; by the 1900s the images were of women shopping, women cooking, women decorating. Men's work was to contribute the money and possibly carry the tree home. Women had become the family repositories of Christmas: they organized and planned, they decorated, shopped, wrapped and cooked. And they also carried the emotional focus of the day.

Christmas dinner was no longer only about the turkey, but was a focus of many traditions, drawing together

---

* This is not something that has faded, either. In 2007, the German National Tourist Office promoted the country's Christmas markets as a destination for those 'tired of commercialism taking over this holiday period' – in other words, if you're tired of commercialism, head for a place that exists to sell things.

commodities and cash transactions, goods and services, and using them as a way to express family connection and love. Families frequently find they have, through a process of repetition and ritual use, imbued commercial, purchased goods with emotion. The 'good' dishes, used only on this day, might be no more expensive than the ones in use daily, but they are good because they were once grandmother's. The ornaments for the Christmas tree might be cheap mass-produced ones, but they are given meaning when parents annually reminisce about buying the ugly neon Santa on their honeymoon as they watch their child hang it up. The order of the events, too – presents on Christmas Eve or Day? Before or after church? Turkey or beef, lunch or dinner? – all these decisions, once repeated, turn cash purchases into emotion. Even watching the same films on television every year becomes part of the ritual. Or it is conversation and jokes: 'it is customary for my father to mention six or seven times how much his wife's relations eat, how much more they come for a visit than his family, and how much money it costs him'.

Such rituals could be both private and communal at the same time. In Germany in the 1920s and 1930s, Christmas Eve became a day for couples to become engaged; radio stations ran an 'Hour for the Betrothed', with background wedding music. In the English-speaking world, nativity plays performed by small children developed for similar reasons in the 1920s and 1930s, as another external expression of the increasing family-centred status of the day.

This focus on family is also visible in the development of Kwanzaa, the holiday of African-American identity created in 1966 by the activist and academic Maulana Karenga. While Chanukah was a minor festival that gained importance owing to its calendrical proximity to Christmas, Kwanzaa was created *ex nihilo* deliberately to coincide with the Christian holiday. Lasting a week from 26 December, its concerns are family and community, each day concentrating on one of seven principles: unity, self-determination, collective responsibility, cooperative economics, purpose, creativity and faith. As in both the Christian and Jewish midwinter holidays, candles are lit (here red, black and green, to represent the African people, their struggle and their deliverance) in a ritual candelabra called a kinara. Again paralleling Christmas and Chanukah, while the purpose is emotive and spiritual, the effect is commercial. Trade fairs are held to supply merchants with Kwanzaa products: cards, books, stationery, mugs and candles, straw mats that symbolize African heritage, drinking cups for ancestral spirits, kente cloth, or shawl-wraps inspired by Ghanaian textiles. Cookery books draw on the culinary traditions of the African diaspora, from the Caribbean and South America as well as Africa and North America, for new 'traditional' Kwanzaa recipes. Magazine articles explain how to produce Kwanzaa decorations, while accompanying advertisements display items to shop for. And again, as with Christmas, people meet to eat, drink and exchange gifts in groups that expand and contract from family to friends to community.

And in all these holidays, family means children: by 1988 just over half of the respondents to a British survey said family was the most important part of the day, while another 18 per cent said it was watching children celebrate (which also must mean family: watching strangers' children has never been a holiday event). Speaking to a Swedish sociologist, one woman made plain the focus: she was 'almost obliged' to go to her daughter's for Christmas Day, she said, as her grandchildren wouldn't feel they'd had 'a proper Christmas if there was no one there as a spectator'. Perhaps domestic Christmas Day customs are like an indoor Macy's parade in miniature – if they aren't observed, there's really no point.

Chapter Twelve

By the twentieth century, the central, most obvious, symbol of the Anglo-American Christmas had become Santa Claus, who continued to evolve to meet changes in society. He travelled by train, and later by plane and car; he used the telegraph to keep track of good children, and soon the telephone too; he was stymied as central-heating reduced the number of chimneys. In 1982, on the cover of the *Saturday Evening Post*, he transferred his ledgers onto a first-generation PC.

Yet however modern he became, he kept his values of 'love and generosity and devotion', against those who 'have been affected by the skepticism of a skeptical age'. That was the response, in 1897, to a letter from an eight-year-old girl to the *New York Sun*, asking if there really was such a person as Santa Claus. Francis Church, the paper's editorial writer, famously replied under the headline, 'Yes, Virginia, there is a Santa Claus', in a column that proved so popular it was reprinted every year until the paper went out of business in 1950.

That is fitting, because business has almost from the start been Santa's business, financing entire newspaper empires with his advertising. Santa sold pipe tobacco, alcohol, fountain pens, breakfast cereal, razors, shaving foam and brushes, soap, socks, soup and spoons. One of the earliest extended campaigns to make use of Santa was that of the Wisconsin-based White Rock mineral-water company, which ran advertisements from 1915 to 1925 showing Santa at home, at work, making deliveries. Although White Rock was merely carbonated water, it was used as a mixer for alcoholic drinks. Gradually, therefore, as the advertisements ran during Prohibition, White Rock became a synonym for alcohol, and Santa reverted to the old Christmas, advertising an adults-only item.

Santa Claus advertises White Rock mineral water in *Life* magazine, December 1923.

As coloured printing became less expensive in the 1880s, Santa's red suit had become the standard, and White Rock's advertisements had reinforced many of the other visual motifs established by Nast: the fur-trimmed jacket, the belt, the boots. From the beginning of the twentieth century, though, one of the most influential series of images of Santa was not an advertisement but the cover of each year's Christmas issue of the *Saturday Evening Post*, America's best-selling journal. J. C. Leyendecker, one of its most successful cover artists, produced a long series of Christmas images, many of which drew on Washington Irvingesque images of the holiday: waits, squires, stagecoaches and other quasi-historical elements. But in 1912 the artist's first Santa for the magazine was unexpectedly modern: not a 'real' Santa at all, but a charity collector dressed up, a thin man wearing a red robe rather than a suit, his everyday trousers visible underneath. Real people dressing up as Santa persisted when Leyendecker's slightly younger colleague, Norman Rockwell, produced his first *Post* cover four years later: a man in a costume shop checks a Santa hat and beard in a mirror as a shop assistant looks on. Later Leyendecker's Santa, like Nast's, went to war, this time in a World War II uniform rather than the stars and stripes, although his leather fly-boy jacket was the now standard red. In contrast to Rockwell and others, Leyendecker's Santa continued to draw on Clement Clark Moore's elf-like creature, and was always less than adult-sized. Rockwell's Santa was the one that embodied the modern archetype: he was fat, bearded, worked at the North Pole, kept ledgers, made toys and crossed the skies above suburban tracts to deliver his gifts.

But nothing did more to influence the image of the gift-bringer than an advertising campaign by Coca-Cola that ran from 1931 to 1964, and again in the 1980s and 1990s. In the campaign's second year, Coca-Cola hired Haddon Sundblom, an American of Swedish descent, who became its principal designer for the next three decades. These advertisements spread, like the drink itself, across the globe, promoting what had become the standard image: a white-bearded man wearing a red jacket trimmed with white fur, belted across a substantial belly, red trousers and black boots and, frequently, a red pointed cap with white fur trim. And Sundblom's Santa was almost always shown in a domestic setting: either at home in the North Pole, or in the homes of those receiving his presents.

Sundblom's Santa popularized Santa's dress and appearance, not because he was the first, or original, but because the advertisements ran for so many years, in so many places. And yet, even as Santa's image became fixed, new details emerged, to become fixed in their turn. One of the most widely recognized changes was barely noticed as such, and many would have sworn that, on the contrary, it had been in place all along. As we saw, the reindeer pulling Santa's sleigh had arrived simultaneously with Santa, in 1821, in *The Children's Friend*. In 1823, in *A Visit from St Nicholas*, Clement Clarke Moore had named them: 'Now, Dasher! Now, Dancer! Now, Prancer, and Vixen! / On, Comet! On, Cupid! On, Dunder and Blixem!'* But of

---

* The Old-Dutch-style spellings of Dunder and Blixem – in modern Dutch, *donder* and *bliksem*, thunder and lightning – soon became rendered more Germanic, as *Donner* and *Blitzen*, possibly owing to the large number of German immigrants in the USA, before ending in a halfway house as Donder and Blixen.

Rudolph there was still no sign: he was only born in 1939, just as the world was about to slide into war once more.

Rudolph was a commercial innovation: in 1939, Robert L. May, a copywriter working for the retail chain Montgomery Ward, produced a pamphlet for customers' children. It began, in couplets following Clement Clarke Moore's rhythms:

> 'Twas the day before Christmas, and all through the hills
> The reindeer were playing, enjoying their spills.

In May's story, the reindeer ostracize their regrettably red-nosed fellow deer:

> Ha ha! Look at Rudolph! His nose is a sight!
> It's red as a beet! Twice as big! Twice as bright!

until one Christmas, Santa's rounds are disrupted by a dense fog. When he stumbles into Rudolph's bedroom and sees his shining nose, he asks him for help, and so, in Ugly Duckling fashion, the story ends with the bullying reindeer watching as

> The funny-faced fellow they always called names,
> And practically never allowed in their games,
>
> Was now to be envied by all, far and near.
> For no greater honour can come to a deer
>
> Than riding with Santa and guiding his sleigh.
> The Number One job, on the Number One day!

The retailer gave away nearly 2.5 million copies, serving its commercial purpose, but the story had no further impact until, ten years later, May's brother-in-law, Johnny Marks, a songwriter, set it to music. It was recorded by

Gene Autry, the 'Singing Cowboy', reached number one in the charts and sold millions.

By this time, the commercial, secular Christmas song had become as important in the American market as secular carols had been in the nineteenth century. By the early decades of the century, the music industry had begun to appreciate the holiday period as a driver of sales: in 1905 one popular vaudeville performer had great success with 'Christmas Time at Pumpkin Center', a sentimental appeal to vanishing rural America. More and more households bought radio sets in the 1920s, increasing the audience for popular music more generally, and seasonal songs in particular, and so professional tune-writers set to work. During World War II such songs made a patriotic contribution, reminding servicemen far away of their families at home. Who knew more about such longings than immigrants and the children of immigrants? Some of the most famous, and most enduring, Christmas hits were therefore written by Jews. In 2014 ASCAP, the organization that collects US songwriters' royalties, produced a list of the twentieth century's most successful holiday songs. No songs from before 1934 made the top thirty, and only two in the top twenty were written after 1959. Of all thirty, half had at least one Jewish contributor, and just three in the top ten were written by Christians.

Meanwhile, Christmas adapted in other ways to wartime, as both sides in the conflict (although not officially atheistic Russia) rewrote aspects of the holiday to support their cause. In 1939, even before the USA had entered the conflict, CBS radio's war correspondent introduced himself: 'from Finland, the country where our legend of Santa Claus and his reindeer first began'. Santa had previously been said to live in an ice palace, sometimes at the North Pole. His new residence in Finland was political, establishing the bona fides of a nation currently being bombed by the Soviet Union, and only weeks away from its establishment as a puppet regime. Similarly, after the German invasion of the Netherlands a Dutch propaganda newsletter included a photograph of St Nicholas visiting the good children of New York. This conflated new Dutch St Nicholas traditions – the mayor of Amsterdam greeting the saint as he arrived from Spain, and parades with Zwarte Piet – which had become popular only in the 1920s, with their wartime ally's own Christmas customs.

Hollywood did its part too. Irving Berlin originally wrote 'White Christmas' as a song about a man in sunny California: 'The sun is shining, the grass is green . . . / There's never been such a day / in Beverly Hills, LA.' Soon, however, the opening was dropped, and it became a song about the lost Christmases of the singer's youth. Then it was included in the wartime film *Holiday Inn*, combined with images of Lincoln and Roosevelt, munitions factories and troops marching off to fight for the right to celebrate Christmas at home: Christmas and patriotism all wrapped up together in a neat holiday package.

German propaganda use of Christmas dated back to the defeat of Germany in World War I. The post-war uprising that led to the dissolution of the German Empire included a *Weihnachtskämpfe*, a Christmas struggle, between the German army and socialist forces on 24 December 1918, helping create the idea in Germany that pre-war Christmases were the real Christmas, while new, modern Christmases were sham, plastic facsimiles. In the 1920s the rising tide of nationalism, with its emphasis on the origins

of the *Volk*, the people, drew together a number of traditions said to be survivals of the real Germany (read,
the undefeated Germany), including 'ancient national
Christmas customs' from the 'age of our primordial
pagan fathers'. At the same time, some innovations of the
twentieth century – electricity, radio, new modern cookers
installed in modern social-housing – were acceptable,
even welcomed, not as novelties in and of themselves, but
as tools to replicate the supposedly ancient rituals of the
holiday: lighting trees, playing carols, cooking traditional
meals. At the same time, some traditions, authentic as
some of them may have been, were diminished. The
Christkind became less prominent than the Weihnachtsmann, a secular figure whose recent arrival – his first
mention was in a poem in 1847 – made him more adapt-
able.

In 1933, the year that Hitler became Chancellor of
Germany, Heinz Steguweit, a World War I veteran and,
from May of that year, a member of the Nazi Party, wrote
Petermann Makes Peace, or, The Parable of German Sacrifice,
rewriting the story of World War I's Christmas truce. In
Steguweit's version, the soldier Petermann erects his tree
behind the trenches to the accompaniment of carols, only
to be killed by an Allied soldier as a sniper shoots out his
tree's lights one by one. The real Christmas, kept alive by
real Germans, ran the not very subtle message, was under
threat.

Yet in reality, Christmas symbols and Christmas ideas
travelled freely across political divides. In the nineteenth
century in Germany, as we saw, many institutions sought
to display some simulation of domesticity at Christmas,
often by erecting a tree. In the USA a more public version

of the tree was created. The first may have been at the 1885 New Orleans Exposition, a decorated fourteen-metre hemlock. In 1912, in Madison Square Park, in New York, a bigger tree – over twenty metres high – formed a dramatic backdrop to a Christmas Eve concert. The idea gained recognition in other cities and towns: by 1914 Austin, Texas had a tree outside its capital building, again a focus for bands, choirs and child-singers. In New York the Madison Square Park tree was replaced first by a tree in Times Square in 1926, and then by one at Rockefeller Center.[*]

Soon the public tree was not about domesticity, but about politics. In the USA it stood as an emblem of the Progressive politics of Theodore Roosevelt and of social reform more generally. Even for those who did not support the political aims of the Progressives, for one night the notion of uniting rich and poor met with general approval. In 1923 the White House moved its tree outside: the tree-lighting, and thus the holiday, had become national, and political, events. In the same decade, in the Weimar Republic, public trees were named *Weihnachtsbäume für alle*, Christmas trees for all those who could not afford their own. Under the Nazis, the tree was reimagined as a survival of the traditions and spirit of the *Volk*. Members of the SA, the Nazi paramilitary unit, took their formal oaths of allegiance beneath them, swearing: 'We promise, on this

[*] The tree at Rockefeller Center dates either from 1933, the first official tree, paid for by the buildings' landlords, or from 1931, while the site was still under construction, when an unlit tree, decorated by the workmen, was erected by their pay-desk. By the end of the twentieth century half a million people visited this tree every weekend.

holy Yule night, to fight tirelessly for the holy struggle of our *Volk*.' The tree was a 'Symbol of National Unity', as each region of the country took turns to send a tree to stand outside the Ministry of Propaganda in Berlin. Across Germany trees were also the spot designated for charitable handouts. In Washington in 1941, a blackout had been imposed after the Japanese attack on Pearl Harbor on 7 December, but the Christmas lighting tradition was considered sufficiently important to morale for the ceremony to go ahead. (In an additional propaganda coup, Churchill was in attendance.)

And so politics has continued to be entwined in the Christmas tree's branches. Every year since 1947 the city of Oslo has sent a tree to London, 'as a token of Norwegian gratitude to the people of London for their assistance during the years 1940–45'.* In 2001 the tree-lighting ceremony at Rockefeller Center became a commemoration of the attack on the World Trade Center three months before, with speeches from the president's wife and the mayor of New York; in 2005, children displaced by Hurricanes Rita and Katrina were given roles in the ceremony.

Other traditional elements of the holiday were also used politically in Germany under the Third Reich. Anti-Semitic newspapers and radio broadcasts inveighed against Jewish department-store owners who were said to commercialize the 'sacred Christmas Day'. Good patriotic citizens were not instructed not to shop, of course, merely to patronize small shops where Christian owners

* And as always, Chanukah won't be left out: the White House began holding an annual menorah-lighting ceremony in 1979; there has been a menorah beside Oslo's tree in Trafalgar Square from 2007.

would ensure the 'holy Christmas holidays' would not be 'desecrated'.

Christmas cards also took on a political slant. The card market had had a bumpy time in the twentieth century. First, the German printers who produced the majority of the cards sold in Britain and the USA lost access to their markets in World War I. After the war, the Depression in the US and the UK, and hyperinflation in Germany, made cards seem a luxury. To counter this, manufacturers and retailers began to promote cards as a way of establishing the right-thinking of the sender. In the 1940s patriotic subjects abounded; after the war was over, cards were sold to benefit UNICEF – the United Nations International Children's Emergency Fund, established to provide food and medicine to children in devastated Europe. Other charities followed their lead, and then so did other fund-raising institutions: museums, galleries, orchestras, scouting and woodcraft groups for children. Good citizens sent good cards.*

 Christmas commerce, too, became an aspect of politics. German seasonal markets were, in the broadest sense, traditional, descendants of the Christmas markets of the fifteenth and sixteenth centuries. But by the mid-twentieth-century many had dwindled to be pale shadows. In both Berlin and Nuremberg, where markets had flourished in the eighteenth century, the few stalls that survived had long

---

* Yet it looks as if this 150-year-old tradition might not survive the electronic world. By the beginning of World War II, the population of England and Wales sent, on average, ten cards each; by 1977, that had risen to eighteen; by 1992, it was twenty-seven. But by 2014, that figure had halved, to fourteen cards per person, the first ever fall in numbers in the history of Christmas cards.

been moved from the city centres to shabby locations in working-class neighbourhoods. These markets now offered no luxuries. At best, customers purchased cheap knick-knacks and souvenirs there before heading to the new retail centres for their bigger purchases. In the first years of Nazi power, however, both Berlin and Nuremberg markets were revitalized, promoted as ideologically superior to the Jewish-owned department stores. In 1933 a new traditional opening ceremony was created for Nuremberg's market, including a Prologue recited by a performer dressed as a *Rauschgoldengel*, the treetop golden angel that had long been manufactured in the city. Berlin followed, its market relocated to a new central site by the nineteenth-century cathedral. This market, too, was presented as a revived custom when Goebbels, Goering and others spoke at the opening ceremony, followed by a parade led by the *Weihnachtsmann*, and the circus-performer Cilly Feindt on a white horse. Carols and the Nazi anthem, 'The Horst Wessel Song', were sung, the tree was lit, and pamphlets outlining the traditions of a 'beautiful *German* Christmas' were distributed.

The Third Reich Christmas was an entirely secular event, and came with a full set of old pagan customs that were so new that they needed to be taught to the general population. The images – the tree, snowy villages, happy families, carols, markets, goose for Christmas dinner – remained essentially the same, while their sharply limited religious content enabled the reshaping of the day as an expression of Germany's new Aryan future, and therefore of the future of the Aryan family. The importance of the holiday to family life was such that when the Nazi Women's League ran courses for *volksdeutsche* women (women of ethnic German descent who had been born and brought up outside Germany), to instruct them in the proper German way of running a household, the subjects included hygiene and health, home decoration and cooking, child-rearing and how to prepare for Christmas: how to make decorations, bake Christmas specialities and sing carols. Yet the alien, modern Anglo-American traditions were not so easily ignored: in 1944, at one Christmas party organized by a German teacher for her *volksdeutche* mothers, an SS officer attended dressed not as the Weihnachtsmann but as Santa Claus.

For Germans, like the Americans and British, had become accustomed to a variety of traditions, and to their amalgamation into a hybrid Christmas, which made them feel as though they were their own, no matter how foreign in origin. This tendency was accelerated by the techno-logical changes of the first half of the twentieth century: by radio, then by film and television. These media innova-tions both spread new habits and made them feel old. Germany's first Christmas Eve radio broadcast, in Berlin in 1924, had a distinctly religious feel: a children's choir sang hymns, and the nativity story was recounted. By 1930 more than 3 million Germans owned a radio, a house-hold object that, according to the manufacturer Siemens, 'brings *Gemütlichkeit* and a happy holiday mood into the home'. Broadcasts followed the pattern of most people's holiday: a religious service (church attendance), children's programmes (family celebrations), Christmas music (a concert) and then dance music (a party). Particular groups were catered for – housewives, or children – as were local interests – stories by local writers, or in regional dialects – while at the same time the idea of a shared heritage was promoted via broadcasts of carols, Bach's *Christmas Oratorio* or Peter Cornelius's *Weihnachtslieder* Christmas song cycle, and Christmas stories and plays by renowned German writers. Broadcasts were structured to enable families to synchronize their activities with the programmes: as well as the Hour for the Betrothed, there was music to unwrap presents by, to dance and sing to, even the recorded sound of matches being struck, for the moment the tree was lit.

Early radio programmes in Britain had a similar institutional slant.* The BBC was granted a monopoly in 1922, and its founding managing director, John Reith, a committed Presbyterian, saw the new technology as an active participant on Christmas Day, a 'loud-speaker' in the festive home. From the very beginning the BBC fabricated new traditions, which were immediately, and most likely unconsciously, presented as though they were ancient. From 1926, *Bethlehem*, a nativity play based on the medieval Chester miracle play, and written by Bernard Walke, the vicar of a parish in Cornwall from 1913 to 1936, was presented annually as 'a link with the past', a broadcast of 'old things and customs', despite being brand new.

Two years later another 'ancient' tradition was first aired. In 1880 the then Bishop of Truro (later the Archbishop of Canterbury), Edward White Benson, had scheduled a Christmas Eve service incorporating carols. It was copied by many churches, including in 1918 by the chapel of King's College, Cambridge, where the dean

---

* The BBC was established in October 1922 by a number of US and UK electrical companies who sold radios and wanted to increase their market by improving the available content. It was taken into public ownership in 1927.

was a former army chaplain committed to extending the congregation of the faithful. As he hoped, the service was extremely popular, and in 1928 the BBC broadcast it, one of a number of Christmas services and concerts it broadcast every December. It broadcast the 1929 service as well, but clearly felt no great commitment to this particular service, omitting it from its 1930 schedule before returning to King's again the following year. Yet somehow by 1931 this thirteen-year-old concert had become considered to be a tradition of the ages, according to the BBC's publicity material; by 1939 it had aged exponentially: 'The festival has been held since the chapel was built nearly 500 years ago'.

By this date, over 34 million people regularly listened to the radio in Britain, out of a population of 47 million. It had become part of the fabric of the nation, and John Reith was determined that it should remain so. The idea of a head of state addressing the nation, if not via the airwaves, was not new. In 1888 George Bernard Shaw was less than impressed by Queen Victoria's Christmas message to Parliament:

> a retired life has left her Majesty rather out of it as to what is actually going on in the world . . . The machine gun massacre of the Sudanese, and the mountain battery cannonade of the unfortunate Thibetans [sic], are indulgently passed over as, respectively 'a brilliant military operation' and 'a disturbance, terminated without difficulty' – quite a Christmassy way of looking at them.

The address via radio was readily recognized as an amplifier for royalty: in 1934 King Haakon VII of Norway broadcast a New Year's Eve speech. Two years earlier in Britain, Christmas had trumped New Year. The first broadcast known as the King's (later Queen's) Christmas speech, although brief and bland to the point of unmemorability, stressed the nature of the holiday: 'I speak now from my home,' the king broadcast 'to all who are celebrating . . . with their children and grandchildren.' In 1933 he addressed 'the members of our world-wide family . . . especially the children', while in 1934 he returned to 'the Festival of the Family'. He repeated the word family seven times that year, home three times, marking a path that is walked to this day, as the words home, family, children, fathers and mothers were repeated over the years, supplemented in wartime with mother country, brotherhood, homecoming, homely and homeland. As war broke out, the monarch assured his people that Christmas was 'above all the festival of peace and of the home', 'above all Children's day', the 'festival of the home', 'this ancient and beloved festival sacred to home', 'the children's festival': a litany of emotive phrases that through this holiday broadcast enabled the twentieth-century British monarchy to present itself as the great promoter of family, home and hearth.*

---

* The continuing process of myth-making can be seen in the film *The King's Speech* (2010), a triumph-over-adversity narrative of George VI's struggles with his stammer against the perceived need to make this annual broadcast in a time of war. While the film portrays his speech as a heart-warming success, at the time one working-class woman wrote in her diary: 'I wish he would not speak'; his broadcast was 'a most uncomfortable quarter of an hour' which she spent 'wishing the whole time that I could do it for him'. How typical she was we cannot know, but this is the kind of voice that the airwaves exist to contradict.

The BBC's own preamble to the speech differed each year – in 1934 the announcer imagined himself to be an 'aerial postman' travelling above the Earth and looking down at each passing country: 'Hello, Brisbane', 'Are you awake, Vancouver?' – a Received Pronunciation Santa on his Christmas rounds. Broadcasts in other years contained profiles of citizens – a 'grand old shepherd', a miner, an island crofter – always a picturesque or quaint type, or employed in non-metropolitan jobs. There were no profiles of ladies working behind the makeup counter at Woolworth's, nor on the assembly line of a car factory, just as Christmas was always a holiday of family togetherness, never, for example, the precipitating factor in an annual peak in divorce rates, or the period when domestic violence rises by a third.

The mythologization of the holiday, and the omniscient, all-seeing narrator looking down on a picture-book world, was not confined to radio. In 1976 a modern commercial version of the Putz came on to the market: miniature ceramic villages, originally produced by a company called Department 56 but quickly copied by many others. Every year, Department 56 produces one or more new 'snow villages'. There is an Alpine Village, a New England Village, a Frost Village, Christmas in the City Village (this city is New York although, unsettlingly, one model is a diner named Night Hawks, based on Edward Hopper's famous painting of anomie and alienation). Dickens features twice, with a Dickens Village and a Dickens Christmas Carol Village. Other manufacturers include regional themes, like the adobe village offered by one California company. Department 56 has just one religious subject, a little town of Bethlehem, among half a dozen film- and television-based villages: *Elf* and *Frozen*, as well as a Grinch village and a Peanuts village. Another company sells a replica of Bedford Falls, the home of the hero of Frank Capra's 1946 film, *It's a Wonderful Life*.

It's a Wonderful Life has become the *Christmas Carol* of the late twentieth- and twenty-first-century holiday. As an idealized, imaginary Tudor Christmas was to the Victorians, so an idealized, imaginary Victorian – a Dickensian – Christmas has become to the twentieth century, and Capra's celluloid 1940s Christmas to the twenty-first: a prism through which to imagine a better, idealized version of ourselves. In these versions, reality and history are mere inconveniences. The first Hollywood talking picture of *A Christmas Carol*, for example, begins with a chorus of 'Hark the Herald Angels Sing', the tune of which was written a dozen years after *A Christmas Carol*, while its opening shot informs viewers that the story was set 'More than a century ago' – five years before Dickens wrote it.

Removing immediacy removes fear. And fear pervades Dickens's *A Christmas Carol* – the fear of starving to death, the fear of a city where 'The ways were foul and narrow; the shops and houses wretched; the people half-naked, drunken, slipshod, ugly. Alleys and archways, like so many cesspools, disgorged their offences of smell, and dirt, and life, upon the straggling streets; and the whole quarter reeked with crime, with filth, and misery.' Instead of Dickens's sole caroller, who is a half-frozen child whose nose is 'gnawed . . . by the hungry cold as bones are gnawed by dogs', Department 56's Dickens Christmas Carol Village offers a jolly outing by the Cratchit family in a sled, the entire family bundled up warmly under rugs, and hats, scarves and mittens. Instead of Dickens's shops where 'Secrets that few would like to scrutinise were bred and hidden in mountains of unseemly rags, masses of corrupted fat, and sepulchres of bones,' Department 56's secondhand shop is freshly painted, and, if a little wonky, charmingly, rather than ominously, so.

The twentieth century saw possibly as many as 500 adaptations of Dickens's novella, and almost without exception they show a better, a happier world, a world of stability and security. Even casting played a part in creating that feeling of stability: between 1934 and 1953 Lionel Barrymore played Scrooge on American radio every year except two. In most of these adaptations, too, Scrooge's nephew Fred fades from view. Without him, the Cratchits are not Scrooge's employees but his surrogate family. Scrooge helps Bob get on in business and provide for his family – a story of social advancement in the Depression.*

A British adaptation in 1935 is blithe and uplifting, as the ragged poor and the guests at the Lord Mayor's banquet come together to sing 'God Save the Queen', all members of a unified society, yet one where everyone knows their place. By contrast, in the 1938 Hollywood version the social world is less hierarchical, more American: the Cratchit house is smallish, but not poverty-stricken; Scrooge presents the turkey to the Cratchits himself rather

---

* In 1922 the playwrights George S. Kaufman and Marc Connelly parodied Tiny Tim's 'God bless us every one', making it Scrooge's company slogan as Tiny Tim Products takes off. And plenty more comedy versions unconsciously replicate the money aspect, instead of reform and charity. *Mickey's Christmas Carol* in 1974 features Scrooge McDuck driving a mini-tractor through his piles of gold; in 1988, *Blackadder's Christmas Carol* makes Ebenezer Blackadder, the family's 'white sheep', 'the kindest, loveliest man in all England', who must learn to be miserly so that his descendants can prosper.

than paying someone to deliver it; Scrooge and Bob, employer and employee, play together in the snow. There is also, in the more religious US, a scene at church, where there is none in the book; Scrooge's reform is demonstrated by sacks of toys rather than food, the holiday spirit a matter of children's pleasure, not appeasing hunger: Andy Hardy does Dickens.

Questioning your place in small-town America was the subtext of *It's a Wonderful Life*, which, although in detail is based on a short story by a novice writer named Philip Van Doren Stern, is essentially another adaptation of *A Christmas Carol*. George Bailey (played by James Stewart) has given up his big-city dreams to protect Bedford Falls from the hard-hearted banker Mr Potter (Lionel Barrymore, playing Scrooge once again, just under another name). When it looks as though the financier will win, destroying George and his family in the process, George contemplates suicide. His guardian angel, Clarence (Henry Travers), intervenes, like the ghosts of Christmas, to show George what Bedford Falls would have been like had he never lived: at the mercy of rapacious capitalism, his brother dead, many others ruined, idyllic Bedford Falls turned into anonymous, uncaring Pottersville. On his return to the present, George, like Scrooge, is transported by the Christmas spirit, running madly through town, wishing all a happy holiday.

The film was released in 1946, and barely made a ripple. The promotional material focused on the small-town location, not the time of year, and it wasn't presented as a holiday film, in part because the genre didn't yet exist. *Holiday Inn* (1942) and *White Christmas* (1954), which bookended Capra's film, possibly created the idea of the

Christmas film, along with *Miracle on 34th Street* (1947). *Holiday Inn* concerned the romantic entanglements of four people, one of whom owns an inn that opens for holidays only: Easter, the Fourth of July, Valentine's Day and so on. The first scene is set on Christmas Eve, the last on New Year's Eve. Irving Berlin's score included 'White Christmas', as well as 'Easter Parade' and 'Be Careful, It's My Heart', which all the critics were sure would be the film's hit song. *Miracle on 34th Street*, by contrast, was set in a big city, New York, at the heart of Christmas commerce, Macy's department store, where Kris Kringle himself (Edmund Gwenn) is hired by the non-believing Doris (Maureen O'Hara) to be the store's resident Santa. His Santa-like generosity is interpreted as mental illness, requiring him to prove in court that he is the 'real' Santa. He does, Doris gives up work to marry and raise a family, and order is restored.

Unlike these films, where the beneficence of modern capitalism is never questioned, the good flourish and the evil suffer, *It's a Wonderful Life* is more truly Dickensian in its acceptance of darkness. George ends happily, like Bob Cratchit, but Potter/Scrooge learns no lessons, and his crimes are never mentioned, much less punished. And so the film languished, and instead the new medium of television reshaped the presentation of Christmas once more. The new genre of the Christmas Special was neither special, in that the shows were old-fashioned variety productions, nor were they particularly Christmassy.

A typical example of the genre was 'One Hour in Wonderland', which was really a teaser for Walt Disney's forthcoming *Alice in Wonderland* feature-length animation. Here Walt Disney himself acted as a party host, with his own family 'welcoming' the guests/performers. Thus, even as a trailer, even with professional entertainers, the programme could superficially appear domestic, for children, and about families, as *Miracle on 34th Street* and *It's a Wonderful Life* had been, with their themes of nostalgia, family, children and giving. Many of the Christmas specials, unlike *Miracle* but like the other films, were set in small towns, as the star 'returned' to his or her roots – Dolly Parton to Tennessee, Anne Murray to Nova Scotia. No stars, apparently, ever came from inner cities, or, if they did, no television executives chose to commission Christmas specials about them. This was an urban and suburban nation preferring to see itself through the lens of rural nostalgia. It was the Bedford Falls that were being celebrated in these televised specials, never the Pottersvilles that most viewers actually lived in.

These shows expounded on themes of altruism, friendship and family. In the 1960s cartoons such as *A Charlie Brown Christmas* (1965) and *How the Grinch Stole Christmas* (1966) stressed warmth over materialism, family over all, *The Grinch* being yet another retelling of the Scrooge story: the Grinch discovering, like Scrooge, that Christmas 'means a little bit more!' Yet with their highly visible inclusion of impedimenta of the holiday – trees, wreaths, food, presents – these programmes presented a paradoxical subliminal message: the need to buy seasonal goods in order to enjoy a holiday whose core message was presented as the unimportance of consumerism.

The increasing visibility of the capitalism that is at the heart of Christmas might be one of the reasons why *It's a Wonderful Life* eventually emerged from obscurity to become one of the most regularly watched, deeply loved Christmas films. The first reason was pure capitalist opportunism: the film's copyright expired in 1974 and it could therefore be broadcast without charge. More importantly, the world had changed since 1946. In the aftermath of World War II there had been, despite the fantasy angel, a bleak realism to the film, with its then-current film-noir camerawork and its narrative of death and despair. In the interim, the camerawork had become nostalgic, while Bedford Falls has since been sanitized into a ceramic 'collectible'. As with adaptations of *A Christmas Carol*, the dark elements have receded into the background, as modern viewers wrap themselves in the nostalgia of a world of skating on a frozen pond, or drugstores where the pharmacist knows everybody's name. Meanwhile the projected horrors of Potter-style capitalism today seem relatively benign. In the dark, alternative reality version of Bedford Falls revealed by the angel, George's wife has become the town's spinster librarian. In a world of twenty-first-century austerity politics, a town where the local library remains open at all still looks like a pretty wonderful life.

Chapter Thirteen

By the twenty-first century Christmas was celebrated by many who shared none of its traditions, who were not even nominally Christian. Magazines, books, film and television have transmitted the formula to places where the meaning of the symbols matters little; their reproduction alone – the Santas, the trees, carols, presents – instead signifying acculturation to a generic Western world, to modernity.

In Japan missionaries had promulgated the religious significance of Christmas from the sixteenth century. As an expression of global popular culture in which Japanese non-Christians might participate, however, Christmas has been, essentially, a twentieth-century phenomenon. By the 1870s some Tokyo shops put up Christmas decorations, but it was only later that the holiday was more widely embraced and reshaped to produce an idiosyncratic Japanese Christmas, a Christmas of decorations, lights, continuous recorded Christmas music, of gifts and shopping, accompanied by Santa Kurosu no ojiisan, Grandfather Santa Claus.

It may be that the holiday was assimilated as easily as it was because the Taoist *oseibo*, or gift-giving season, falls at the end of the year, for the Japanese Christmas is a holiday of consumption without qualification. On the streets, music is piped from shops; more music plays inside: 'Jingle Bells' is a perennial favourite and local pop groups also produce their own holiday-themed songs. As in the West, department stores welcome Santas, who take orders for gifts and display nativity scenes or other holiday set-pieces. Outside, brightly lit trees are everywhere. (If not always conventionally decorated: one Tokyo shopping centre has had a Godzilla Christmas tree.)

The Western emphasis on the holiday as one of family and, especially, of children, however, is absent. Instead, Christmas togetherness is interpreted as the equivalent of Valentine's Day, a day for young couples. Just as pre-summer advertising in the West sternly reminds young women how many days remain for them to acquire a 'beach-ready body', so one Japanese Christmas beauty salon has gloomily promised, 'You can definitely become beautiful by Christmas'. Other advertisements use tag-lines such as 'Silent Night' to provide a Christmas flavour, but the words' actual meaning, and historical context, become incidental. One advertisement showing champagne and chocolates was captioned 'Silent night's sweet message to him', while the phrase 'Holy night' has come to mean an evening when couples go out for dinner, exchange gifts and stay overnight at a hotel.

Christmas has assimilated traditions from half a dozen cultures and countries, and therefore appears endlessly flexible. Yet the transgressive impact of these advertisements on Westerners, the feeling of sheer wrongness that they invoke, makes it clear that this flexible holiday in reality has many firm, if unspoken, rules. For example, a study undertaken in Indiana in the 1970s explored what its author called the 'Tree Rule'. None of the people questioned had any idea that they followed this rule, or even that there were any rules concerning Christmas trees. Nonetheless,

— Married couples with children of any age put up trees;

— Unmarried couples without children do not put up trees;

— Single parents, the widowed and the divorced, with children, may put up trees, but are not obliged to.

Of those surveyed, 90 per cent adhered to this pattern, and the 10 per cent who did not always provided extenuating circumstances for their dereliction: absence from home, ill-health and the like.*

Many other traditions of the day have similar unspoken rules, even for those – or possibly especially for those – elements so often dismissed as new or materialistic. These rules ensure that what appears commercial nevertheless also plays a more profound role, that of strengthening social networks. In the Indiana study, those surveyed were clear that, if gifts were sent by post, they had to be double wrapped – that is, they were first gift-wrapped, and then parcelled up in outer wrappings, so that the present could be ceremoniously unwrapped at the appropriate time, after the outer wrapping had been removed. But only 10 per

---

* More than a century earlier, also in Indiana, although Christmas trees had then only recently arrived in the Midwest, the banker Calvin Fletcher followed the Tree Rule too, erecting a tree at home when his children were young; once they were grown, the tree moved to the houses where his grandchildren lived.

cent of gifts were not handed over personally. The great majority were ceremonially opened at home.* Nine-tenths of gifts were from adults to children under eighteen, and just a tenth were received by adults. This lack of reciprocity was mirrored, too, in value; two-thirds of gifts to adults from children were of nominal value. The survey found, however, that as gifts were given to more distant relatives, or to friends and acquaintances, reciprocity of quantity and value were more generally expected and quantified.

The nature of giving, and of expectations, had changed once Santa became a department-store regular. Children had initially received improving gifts, before these gave way to toys selected to reflect what parents believed their children might like, or at least ought to like. But when children were sitting on Santa's lap and listing out their desires, gifts were no longer expressions of parental hopes, expectations or affection for their children. The children were now, if at one remove, shopping, actively engaged in the culture of consumerism.

This culture of consumerism is a two-way street. Items are purchased, but then can become a reservoir of nostalgia, not commodity. In Sweden, for example, a much-loved 1947 children's book, *Johans Jul* (Johan's Christmas), by the journalist Eva von Zweigbergk, has become for many a blueprint to follow to create a 'proper' old-fashioned Christmas. To others, film and television provide templates, whether it is Americans longing for Bedford Falls, or

---

* Of course, 'home' is a fluid term. In one Swedish survey, 80 per cent said they spent Christmas Eve 'at home', yet 61 per cent of households reported six people or more were present at their Christmas Eve, in a country where the average number of people per household is fractionally over 2.

Swedes recalling 'a real *Fanny and Alexander* Christmas', a fictional early twentieth-century setting created by Ingmar Bergman in a 1982 television drama.

As books, magazines and newspapers, then film and television, have led to a standardization of our symbols and traditions, they have also spread them across international borders. The hand-carved nutcrackers of the Erzgebirge mountains in the Germany of the nineteenth century achieved national fame in a tale by a middle-class state bureaucrat, E. T. A. Hoffmann's *The Nutcracker and the Mouse-King* (1816), which in 1844 was adapted by the Frenchman Alexandre Dumas, from which choreographers Marius Petipa and Lev Ivanov and composer Pyotr Ilyich Tchaikovsky created the ballet *The Nutcracker* for Russia's Mariinsky Theatre in 1892.

This production was only mildly acclaimed, and Tchaikovsky condensed his score into an orchestral piece, *The Nutcracker Suite*, which was initially to prove far more successful, travelling the world. So too did a child christened Giorgi Melitonovitch Balanchivadze, who trained at the Mariinsky before fleeing the Russian Revolution and being reborn in Paris, and then New York, as the choreographer George Balanchine. In 1944 Willam Christensen, founder of the San Francisco Ballet, drew on the memories of Balanchine and of his fellow dance-exile Alexandra Danilova to stage the first American *Nutcracker*.[*] Ten years later Balanchine, by then the founder of the New York City Ballet, choreographed his own version.

From Germany to France, from France to Russia, from

---

[*] Possibly some of the impetus came from Disney's 1940 film *Fantasia*, which used Tchaikovsky's suite to great effect.

Russia to the USA, the story evolved at each step. Yet in all these versions *The Nutcracker* captured the essence of Christmas: a piece with a formal structure, like the rituals of Christmas, which nonetheless seethed with the emotions of family love and family discord even as it highlighted the magic of childhood and of childhood toys. In the ballet's new home in New York, Balanchine insisted on a giant tree onstage. 'The ballet *is* the tree,' he proclaimed, just as the Rockefeller Center tree represented Christmas to New Yorkers outdoors. In 1957 and 1958 *The Nutcracker* reached its largest public to date, transmitted on US television. It tapped into the burgeoning Christmas broadcast tradition and, like those programmes, encompassed via greenery, wintry scenes, family and children, gifts and giving, a Christmas spirit without Christianity.

In the twenty-first century, virtually every ballet company in the USA, and many outside it, rely on Christmas *Nutcracker* audiences for their annual profits. In the foyers they sell *Nutcracker* T-shirts, *Nutcracker* jigsaws or *Nutcracker* jewellery boxes with little revolving dancers on top. There are Disney Mickey and Minnie Mouse versions of *Nutcracker* characters, and Barbie and Ken dolls in *Nutcracker* costumes, a Winnie-the-Pooh *Nutcracker* and the Starbucks *Nutcracker* 'Bearista'. In turn, many of these trade-name, branded *Nutcracker* versions of the characters have been adapted into – what else? – Christmas tree ornaments and decorations.

It is these contrasts, and these changes – from the whittler in the Erzgebirge mountains to the media corporation commodity – that make Christmas what it is: a holiday that shape-shifts, that transforms itself, to become what we – what our cultures – need it to be at any given time. Even when we can trace a single line of descent for a tradition, the underpinnings of each detail, or the emotions attached to it, can be dramatically at odds. Santa is benevolent and, in venturing into our houses, drinking the odd cup of tea or eating a biscuit or two that have been left out for him, he is domesticated. He is not Odin or Freya, leading the Wild Hunt across the winter sky. Nor is he the Christmas monster, the Joulustaalo of Lapland, using his silver knife to disembowel and devour families.*

Yet while we have tamed so much, a little fear always lurks in 'winter's tales' with their 'spirits and ghosts . . . that glide by night'. No one quite knows why winter, and Christmas more specifically, became the time of ghost stories. According to Shakespeare, Christmas is the sole time of year when 'no spirit can walk abroad' and 'No fairy . . . nor witch hath power to charm'. Perhaps 'So hallowed' a day gave immunity, allowing people to speak of the things that otherwise frightened them.

For whatever reason, the connection has been strong: a 1658 'history of apparitions, oracles, prophecies, and predictions' includes five tales that link ghosts and ghostly

---

* Nor is he even a descendant of Siberian shamans, an enticing 1980s theory that suggested Santa's origins were found in these men who, in trances instigated by the consumption of fly-agaric mushrooms, wore red and white robes, flew through the air in sleighs guarded by reindeer spirits and entered houses through their smoke-holes. Sadly, Siberian shamans were later discovered not to travel by sleigh in trances, to have little or nothing to do with reindeer spirits, nor to wear red and white, nor descend through smoke-holes.

happenings to the holiday, although by 1730, telling ghost stories was considered nothing more than a seasonal pastime of 'Countryfolks'. The nineteenth-century love of antiquarianism brought ghost stories back into the mainstream. Walter Scott promised holiday tales of 'conjuror and ghost, / Goblin and witch', while the centrepiece of the Dingley Dell Christmas celebrations in *The Pickwick Papers* was the retelling of a story of goblins, and was published, of course, just in time for a story of Christmas ghosts to be read at Christmas.

Perhaps it was the absolute domestication of the holiday that made these stories so popular. Just as living in safe societies makes reading crime fiction pleasurable rather than unnerving, so perhaps sitting comfortably, sipping a hot drink while the children break their new toys around you, makes ghostly apparitions enjoyable rather than frightening. The comic writer Jerome K. Jerome did wonder how 'Whenever five or six English-speaking people meet round a fire on Christmas Eve, they start telling each other ghost stories . . . It is a genial, festive season, and [yet] we love to muse upon graves, and dead bodies, and murders, and blood.' And this continues today, with an entire genre of gory Christmas-themed horror films.

The antithesis of Christmas, whether by slasher films or simply by complaining of the horrors of the season, had by the end of the nineteenth century become an industry in itself, as those writers and artists who felt so inclined found plenty of commercial outlets for their bile. Much of this was comic. In George and Weedon Grossmith's *Diary of a Nobody* (1892), that masterpiece of British lower-middle-class suburban life, one character declares:

I hate a family gathering at Christmas. What does it mean? Why, someone says: 'Ah! we miss poor Uncle James, who was here last year', and we all begin to snivel . . . Then another gloomy relation says: 'Ah! I wonder whose turn it will be next?' Then we all snivel again, and proceed to eat and drink too much.

George Bernard Shaw hated more widely and ferociously, although with an undertow of knowingness, a we-are-all-in-this-together comedic turn to his spleen. Christmas, he ranted,

> is an indecent subject; a cruel, gluttonous subject; a drunken, disorderly subject; a wasteful, disastrous subject; a wicked, cadging, lying, filthy, blasphemous, and demoralizing subject . . . on its own merits it would wither and shrivel in the fiery breath of universal hatred; and anyone who looked back to it would be turned into a pillar of greasy sausages.

Others saw no humour in their hatred. The usually feral Ambrose Bierce was fairly subdued about the holiday, Christmas being merely 'A day set apart and consecrated to gluttony, drunkenness, maudlin sentiment, gift-taking, public dulness and domestic behavior.' Contrast that to the poet Philip Larkin back in England: 'this Christmas idiocy bursts upon one like a slavering Niagara of nonsense . . . seeing your house given over to hordes of mannerless middle class brats and your good food & drink vanishing into the quacking tooth-equipped jaws of their alleged parents'. (It is the 'alleged' that makes this perhaps the nastiest Christmas tirade on record.) Just as the clerics of the first millennium condemning drinking and dancing revealed that this was what was occurring, so these twentieth-century misanthropes fulminating against the holiday show how much the holiday means to the majority. If Christmas mattered as little, were as universally disliked as these naysayers suggest, no one would have paid them to say nay.

Consider the Christmas markets established in the South Tyrol in the 1960s and 1970s with the enthusiastic support of the Italian national tourist agency. Historically the region had once been part of Habsburg Austria; today more than half the population is German-speaking. The introduction of German-style markets was not, therefore, a simple intrusion of an alien culture. And in this tourist area, these new old markets were a commercial success, but the complaints they generated are telling. The markets were too commercial, it was said; they were too secular; or possibly too historic. Whichever 'too' they exhibited, what they embodied was a conflict between a venue that was historically authentic, yet at the same time offered items that people wanted to buy. If they were too historically accurate, they lost their customers; if the sellers stocked the contemporary merchandise their customers wanted, they were decried as little different from a shopping centre. The inherent contradiction they embodied was the desire to create an illusory world that people might inhabit for a little while, yet one that functioned to modern commercial standards.

There were two solutions to this dilemma. The modern Christmas nostalgists rejected the Christmas of the recent past – no Santa, no Dickens, no Irving, no tree. Their aim was an authenticity found by uncovering ever-earlier practices and customs. One British Christmas anthology published shortly after World War I took pride in rejecting nineteenth-century carols, Yule logs, snowy scenes and 'jovial Squires'. Even robins found a place on its hate-list. No Washington Irving ('tedious'), nor Pepys ('about as rare and secret as the Piccadilly Tube'). To such Christmas originalists, the 'real' Christmas was precisely that, 'rare' and 'secret', its appeal located in its very lack of comforting familiarity sought by the majority. The Christmas of the masses, by contrast, was a holiday of largely recent traditions, be they turkey, or goose and red cabbage, or a tree, presents, watching *It's a Wonderful Life*, singing carols or playing Duke Ellington's *Nutcracker Suite*, or Nat King Cole's 'Chestnuts Roasting in a Open Fire', or in Britain listening to the Queen's Speech or the carol concert from King's.

For, while Christmas has transformed itself over the centuries, from a time for the nobility to display their wealth to their dependants, to a time for adults to enjoy what little extra they could gather, to a festival primarily for and about children – from elite to mass, from adult to child, from public to family – while the holiday has altered, it has survived, it has thrived, because, ultimately, Christmas is not what is, or even has been, but what we hope for.

Part of the meaning of Christmas is in repetition, but a very particular form of repetition, a repetition of forgetting and remembering, of remembering and misremembering. The early twentieth-century journalist G. K. Chesterton wrote dozens of pieces on the holiday, one of which was a story entitled 'The Shop of Ghosts'. In a shabby London shop, an 'old and broken' white-bearded proprietor refuses all payment for the toys he stocks, prompting the narrator to recognize him as Father Christmas, just as another customer enters, none other than

Charles Dickens, to whom Father Christmas confides that he is dying. Dickens waves it away: 'Dash it all, you were dying in my time.' The next customer is the eighteenth-century essayist Sir Richard Steele, who is also astonished by the old man's complaint, 'for the man was dying when we wrote about Sir Roger de Coverley and his Christmas'. So too with Ben Jonson, who remembers Father Christmas's failing health in the seventeenth century. Finally 'a green-clad man, like Robin Hood' wonders at the phenomenon that is Father Christmas: 'I [also] saw the man dying', he remembers before it is given to Dickens to comprehend the greater truth: 'Mr Dickens took off his hat with a flourish . . . "I understand it now," he cried, "you will never die."'

It is this cycle of death and renewal that is the heart of Christmas. It allows us an illusion of stability, of long-established communities, a way to believe in an imagined past, when it was safe for children to play in the street, when no one locked their doors and everybody knew their neighbours, all the while unconsciously omitting the less desirable parts of those times. In our imagined past, we can vicariously enjoy Jane Carlyle's Christmas party romp while remaining oblivious to Hannah Cullwick's back-breaking, filthy eighteen-hour work-days. We can imagine the taste of home-grown and home-preserved vegetables while overlooking the miles trudged carrying buckets of water, or weeding in the blazing sun, or fear of a drought that would bring starvation.

The stories of family holidays of the past are similarly misted and softened, the edges smoothed away unconsciously. Psychologists studying the function of memory have found that, over time and over generations, distressing or embarrassing elements in the retelling of family events vanish; incidents that have no physical or emotional meaning to the next generation are forgotten; details that are unfamiliar to their audiences are replaced by more familiar details from their own lives. We can see how this has regularly occurred in Christmas celebrations in every country. When people say they miss the old holiday traditions, few mean that they miss people creeping up on their house and firing guns in the middle of the night. Or that they miss wearing goat-skeletons on their heads. Or that they miss Christmas being the one day in the year that they can afford to eat meat.

What they mean is that they miss what we understand emotively to be the central core of the holiday, not the lives we have, but the lives we would like to have, in a world where family, religion, personal and social relationships are built on firm foundations. It is not, therefore, surprising that the most profound changes in the celebration of Christmas accompanied the four great revolutions of the modern period in the West: the Civil War that toppled Charles I and brought Cromwell to power, the American Revolution, the French Revolution and the Industrial Revolution. These revolutions brought changes that were irreversible. Industrialization, modernization, urbanization: all contributed to a communal desire for the past, for a place and a time that never existed, where we are loved, protected and cherished.

The rituals of Christmas allow us to believe, if only for one day a year, that that world exists. And the real magic? By repeating the rituals, we can go back there every year. Christmas nostalgia is not only for the Christmases of our childhoods, or those we have read about, or seen in films and television. It is a conflation of all of those Christmases, a pick-and-mix collection of traditions, emotions and rituals. Some are ours, some our parents', or what we think we remember of what our parents have recalled of their own childhood Christmases. Others come from books, from magazines, from how Martha Stewart or Nigella Lawson or the Food Network or Oprah tells us things have 'always' been done, validating our own, or brand-new, customs by claiming that they are long-standing rituals based in historical reality.

'Ceremony', wrote a seventeenth-century historian, 'keeps up all things; 'Tis like a Penny-Glass to a rich Spirit, or some excellent Water; without it the Water were spilt, the Spirit lost.' So do our inexpensive Christmas containers, our rituals and traditions, enable us to savour the rich emotions and values that lie within.

Ultimately, we need to believe that Christmas is, as Scrooge's nephew Fred tells him

> a good time; a kind, forgiving, charitable, pleasant time; the only time I know of, in the long calendar of the year, when men and women seem by one consent to open their shut-up hearts freely, and to think of people below them as if they really were fellow-passengers to the grave, and not another race of creatures bound on other journeys. And therefore, uncle, though it has never put a scrap of gold or silver in my pocket, I believe that it *has* done me good, and *will* do me good; and I say, God bless it!

Further Reading

In the last forty years, Christmas has started to be taken seriously as a subject. There are now many academic books, and some more general introductions. Good overviews are Mark Connelly, *Christmas: A History* (2012) and Paul Frodsham, *From Stonehenge to Santa Claus: The Evolution of Christmas* (2008).

For Christmas in Britain, the standards are J. M. Golby and A. W. Purdue, *The Making of Modern Christmas* (2000); J. A. R. Pimlott, *The Englishman's Christmas: A Social History* (1978); and Gavin Weightman and Steve Humphries, *Christmas Past* (1987). Some of these are now somewhat out of date, but they remain important. The sections on Christmas in Ronald Hutton's *The Stations of the Sun: A History of the Ritual Year in Britain* (1996) are essential reading too.

For Christmas in Germany, books in English include Karin Friedrich (ed.), *Festive Culture in Germany and Europe from the Sixteenth to the Twentieth Century* (2000) and, especially, the magisterial Joe Perry, *Christmas in Germany: A Cultural History* (2010).

Among the many books on Christmas in the USA, Karal Ann Marling, *Merry Christmas! Celebrating America's Greatest Holiday* (2000) takes an original and innovative look at various customs. Stephen Nissenbaum, *The Battle for Christmas* (1996) and Penne L. Restad, *Christmas in America: A History* (1995) are both highly recommended, especially for their use of diaries, letters and other original sources.

For those with a sociological bent, Daniel Miller (ed.), *Unwrapping Christmas* (1993) is the standard work on how, what and why we do what we do on the day.

The origins of the Christmas tree are neatly summarized by Bernd Brunner, *Inventing the Christmas Tree*, trans. Benjamin A. Smith (2012); and the leading expert on Santa and St Nicholas remains Charles W. Jones, *Saint Nicholas of Myra, Bari, and Manhattan: Biography of a Legend* (1978).

For further reading on the fluidity of custom and tradition, the introduction in Svetlana Boym, *The Future of Nostalgia* (2010) has never been surpassed. Eric Hobsbawm and Terence Ranger (eds.), *The Invention of Tradition* (1983), while not dealing with Christmas as such, have much to say on history and how we read it.

A complete reading list, together with full notes on all the sources used in this book, appears online, at:

www.christmas-biography.com

Clive Barda

JUDITH FLANDERS is a *New York Times* bestselling author and one of the foremost social historians of the Victorian era. She is a frequent contributor to *The Wall Street Journal*, *The Daily Telegraph*, and *The Times Literary Supplement*. She lives in London.